BRAIN
BUZZED

**39 Fascinating, Surprising, Useful Discoveries
From Science About How Our Minds Work**

Marlin M. Cluts

Disclaimer: No attempt has been made to critique the science studies referenced. However, the author believes all sources to be reliable.

Book Design by www.Delaney-Designs.com
Copy Editing by Vanessa Ta

Paperback Edition ISBN 978-0-578-75724-7

Web site: www.brainbuzzed.com

PREFACE

I'm not a neurosurgeon or even a neuroscientist, so you won't see many technical terms. But I do have a doctorate degree (EdD) in Instructional Technology with a specialization in Human Performance Technology. I also spent 38 years in the business world, retiring as CEO of a commercial bank. That means I have a practical interest in how people accomplish work and attain their personal goals.

I am struck by how often we say we believe certain facts, but we do things to the contrary. In fact, in the world of Human Performance Technology, Chris Argyris coined the term "espoused theories" to apply to a set of assumptions we'd like to be true about how we work, and the term "theories in use" for those rules that seem to actually govern our behavior. They are usually quite different. Argyris was referring the business world, but I've found the same principle applies to our everyday lives.

That concept was the jumping point for my search of brain science. I found anomalies in how our brain works, and plenty of facts running contrary to our intuition. But the research also led me to new discoveries revealing our brains are much more malleable than we thought. In recent years scientists have found that our brains can *physically* change, even from just thoughts. So I've included relevant studies as well.

Over the years I've collected hundreds of articles and books about these unexpected facts. The 39 brief chapters in the book summarize the most useful.

Forgive me if my business background makes me overly brief in the chapters. They are short and concise and cover a variety of topics. But I have provided references for further study if you wish.

I hope you enjoy.

CONTENTS

INTRODUCTION

"You have power over your mind—not outside events.
Realize this and you will find strength."
—Marcus Aurelius, Roman emperor from 161 to 180 AD

Imagine a professional football stadium filled with spaghetti.

That's a lot of pasta, right? But imagine all that spaghetti is crammed into the human skull. It would be a rough representation of the myriad electrical pathways and potential connections in our minds.

Yet this visualization is magnitudes short on scale and does nothing to signify complexity.[1]

It's been called the most complex, magnificent entity in the universe. And it changes itself. Our brains physically transform and evolve, not only from external stimuli, but also in reaction to our own thoughts.

Yet despite this marvelous ability, our brains have not kept pace with the complexity of the modern world. For example, parts of our brain evolved in pre-historic times to detect patterns, like dangerous corners where tigers lurked. Today, with few tigers running loose, these same circuits give us false signals. But we can train the reasoning part of our brains to recognize these false signals and mediate their impact. Becoming aware of these errant signals is an important first step to counteract them. Specific actions are also possible as we will discuss in the chapters.

Better yet, our brains can change in ways we never thought possible. And the means to nurture and cultivate such transformations are within reach.

Consider the internet when it was first introduced. It was available only to academics and the elite. But over time, it became available to the masses. Now it's in homes all around the world.

We are at a similar stage in the new brain science. Originally only available to academics and researchers, the new science of our most valuable tool is now readily accessible. Prospects are intriguing, but most of the world still operates under old paradigms.

The following chapters explore thirty-nine fascinating and fun facts about how our minds work, contrary to many of our typical assumptions. The new science and resulting understanding can be liberating and useful in our everyday lives, at home and at work.

The thirty-nine chapters of this book have been written as brief overviews summarizing over a hundred articles and books. Some are for fun, but most are practical. In fact, chapters were selected primarily for utility.

Some are just little things. But learning to recognize those little things can lead to a more satisfying, productive life.

References and recommended reading are also provided for further study.

The book is divided into two main parts:

1. **How our brain fools us.** We make better decisions and make more sense of our complex world by understanding our brain's idiosyncrasies. Part One offers insight into recognizing and dealing with these issues.

2. **How our brain changes.** Our constantly changing brain presents an immense opportunity. We can direct how our minds change and develop traits and skills previously considered untrainable. Our minds are much more malleable than we thought. Part Two offers specific examples and ways to induce beneficial brain changes.

Part One is ordered in no specific sequence, so feel free to jump to areas of interest. In Part Two, chapters 19 through 25 build upon each other so you may find it more satisfying to read them in order. Otherwise, feel free to skip around in Part Two as well.

PART ONE

How Our Brain Fools Us

"Everything we hear is an opinion, not a fact.
Everything we see is a perspective, not the truth."

—Marcus Aurelius

1. Patterns Where None Exist

Scientists have found a module in the left hemisphere of the brain that drives humans to search for a pattern or causal relationship, even when there is no such thing.[2]

Imagine you are participating in an experiment where you're shown a sequence of flashing lights colored either green or red. You're shown several sequences of twenty. Your job is to predict the color of the next flash of light, and you will receive a score on the accuracy of your predictions.

Oh, and you will be competing with pigeons.

Here are a couple of typical sequences:

RGRGGGGGRGGGGRGGGGGG

RRGGGGGRGGRGGGGGGGGGG

Scientists arranged the flashes to be random but always with green flashing 80 percent of the time and red just 20 percent of the time.

How would you have done?

Scientists found rats or pigeons, when rewarded for correctly guessing the right color, quickly learned the best strategy: guess green every time, guaranteeing an 80 percent success rate.

But humans didn't do nearly as well. Instead of picking green every time, they got caught up trying to guess the next red flash. On average, they scored only 68 percent instead of locking in the 80 percent by sticking with green. And they often performed worse the longer they tried, because they thought they'd discovered the "pattern" among purely random flashes.[3]

But what about the humans in that experiment? Were they just misled or were they outside of normal in some way?

Let's try the really brainy people of Yale.

Philip Tetlock in his book *Expert Political Judgment: How Good Is It? How Can We Know?* describes an incident he witnessed thirty years ago in a Yale classroom. Rats were put in a T-shaped maze and food was placed in either the left or right path of the top of the T. The food was switched on a random basis but on the left 60 percent of the time and on the right 40 percent of the time. Students were asked to predict on which side of the T the food would appear. The rats eventually figured out the food was on the left more often and almost always went left, scoring nearly 60 percent. The students, with a Yale pedigree and reputation to protect, searched for hidden order in the food placements, yielding a mere 52 percent. The rats, not worrying about their reputation, were not embarrassed by being wrong two out of every five tries. But the Yale students could not accept a 40 percent error rate so they "patterned" a 50 percent error rate instead.

Another example will appeal to sports fans. Have you ever watched a basketball game where one player gets "hot," scoring multiple baskets in a short time-frame?

In the final seconds of the game, the crowd screams to get the ball to the hot player for the winning basket, feeling the player is "in the zone." Are they right?

A survey of basketball fans showed that 91 percent thought the "hot" player was more likely to make a basket. Likewise, they thought a "cold" player (having missed the last two or three shots), was less likely to score. Eighty-four percent felt the ball should be passed to a player who had just made a couple shots in a row.[4]

But there is a problem. There is no such thing as a "hot" hand.[5]

Psychologists studied shooting statistics of the Boston Celtics and Philadelphia 76ers for the 1980 to 1981 season and could find no evidence to support the hot hand theory. For the theory to be correct, statistics should show a greater probability of making a basket after having made two or three in a row. But when the scientists analyzed the data, they found that just wasn't the case.

Let's zero in on Julius Erving (aka "Dr. J." who was a superstar for the Philadelphia 76ers). After he had made two baskets in a row, his probability of making the next basket was 52 percent. His probability after two misses was 51 percent. If he made three in a row, his next one went in 48 percent of the time. If he missed three in a row, he scored on the next attempt 52 percent of the time. In short, the probability of success was about 50 percent regardless of prior results. Supporting the data, other players yielded similar "patterns."[6]

In another pattern experiment, participant teachers were asked to either reward students' punctuality or punish their tardiness over a fifteen-day period. For example, punishment could be such things as after school retention or an unwanted assignment. Positive reinforcement could be earning points toward pizza or an early dismissal or just recognition. The question was whether the "carrot" or the "stick" worked best. The teachers' verdict was the "stick." But the experiment had been rigged. In reality, students arrived at random times generated by computer, unrelated to the reward or punishment exacted by teachers.[7]

Yet the teachers were convinced their interventions had an effect.

Just like the Yale students who perceived "patterns" in the rat food placement, and the crowd sensing the "hot" player, the teachers observed patterns that were not real.

This pattern-recognition part of our brain can be troublesome:

1. It leaps to conclusions or overestimates causality. *Two in a row of almost anything, such as rising stock prices or rolls of the dice, will make us expect a third.*

2. It is unconscious. *Even if we think we are being analytic, our pattern-seeking brain may guide us to a more instinctive decision.*

3. It is automatic. *Whenever we are confronted with something random, we will search for patterns within it. Our brain was built for this from our ancestors' hunting and gathering times.*

4. It is uncontrollable. *We can't turn it off.*[8]

Savvy marketing people understand this behavior well. Consider the design of slot machines, where a pull of the handle often results in a pair of jackpot icons on the first two reels while the gambler waits breathlessly for the third wheel to stop on the same icon.[9] A commission-oriented stock broker will point out the stock has been up two days in a row. "Better get in now." Or a retail sales person, "We've sold out two days in a row. Get it now."

We were designed to expect patterns. Nature itself yields many examples, such as thunder following lightning. Our brain learned these patterns and created corresponding expectations. But in a modern, complex world, many events are just random and not patterns at all, such as the "hot dice" or "hot stock."

So how can we differentiate between a pattern or random information? Or, what can we do to break this ingrained pattern problem?

Statistics can help. We rely on statistical models for weather forecasts, and statistical results are key in the approval of medical procedures and drugs. But with pattern recognition issues, we must beware of *irrelevant* statistics. It's even possible to see patterns in statistics that are really just random.

Consider David Leinweber, who wondered what statistics would best predict the performance of the US stock market from 1981 through 1993. He combed through mounds of data and found one that would forecast with 75 percent accuracy: the amount of butter produced each year in Bangladesh! And he said he could improve the accuracy to 99 percent by including the number of sheep in the U.S.![10] Obviously, this is a laughable correlation and a random fluke. We must be sure there is a causative affect in the statistics.

So what *should* we do?

For one, just knowing we have pattern recognition problems helps.

But a simple method can free us from such fallacies. An experiment at Carnegie Mellon University showed that people will intuitively bet on "tails" after a coin flip has come up "heads" several times in a row, thinking tails is "due." But if researchers let the coin "rest" for a while between flips, participants would often bet heads again—as if the passage of time allowed the coin to revert to its true 50/50 chance of being either![11] The truth is it was the participants who benefited from the break in the action.

While the coin flip example is comical, taking a rest is one of the best ways to disengage our pattern-seeking brain.

In summary, when we make decisions or form opinions, we need to ask ourselves if we are seeing patterns that are just not there in the data or behavior. In such situations we need to consider the availability of better data or statistics. Or in more immediate situations we can divert ourselves with another activity for twenty minutes or so.[12] That should give us a fresh perspective.

2. Brain Shortcuts

Our brain creates filters or shortcuts to avoid tedious processing.
That's usually a good thing. But the same process can lead to trouble.

Try reading the following:

I cdnuolt blveiee taht I cluod aulacity uesdnatnrd waht I was rdanieg. Tnahks to the phaonmneal pweor of the hmuan mnid, aoccdrnig to rscheearchres at Cmabrigde Uinervtisy, it dseno't mtaetr in what oerdr the ltteres in a wrod are, the olny iproamtnt tihng is taht the frsit and lsat ltteer be in the rghit pclae.

Despite the words above being absurdly misspelled, chances are you were able to understand the whole thing. That's because over your years of reading, your brain has developed shortcuts to spare itself from processing every single letter of a word.

In this case, that's a blessing, because it makes your reading quicker and easier.

But mental shortcuts also have their disadvantages as well. To experience one for yourself, watch a short video about selective attention at Youtube.com. Search for "Selective Attention Test from Simon and Chabris (1999)"; when you're done, continue reading.

Did you spot the gorilla brazenly walking across the room—and even pausing to beat his chest—as the players passed around the basketball?

If you didn't, you're not alone. About 50 percent of viewers are so focused on counting passes that they entirely miss the ape.

And if something that big and hairy can be overlooked, it's worth considering how many other times our reliance on mental shortcuts to breeze through our daily routines is blinding us to the extraordinary.

Want to test yourself again? Try watching the spin-off video. Go to Youtube.com and search "Selective Attention Test 2.0"; when you are done, continue reading.

Almost everyone spots the gorilla tackling the banana.

But almost no one notices the dancing chicken.

That's in part because the latter video has more going on than the previous one, but it's also because it plays on your brain's tendency to create shortcuts that focus on the familiar and expected. The previous video trained you to look out for a gorilla, so this time you spotted the banana while it acted like an ape by beating its chest, and then the actual gorilla, but at the expense of seeing something that was entirely new.

Let's apply this principal to something more familiar than gorillas or chickens. Have you ever looked for the jar of mayonnaise in the refrigerator and couldn't find it? Then you called your spouse, parent, or roommate over only to have them spot it right in front of your nose?

Chances are your brain's filtering mechanisms were active because the scene before you was all too familiar.

Here's how to find the mayonnaise. Try a different perspective. Take a step to the side, kneel, or maybe step up on a stool. You will have a less familiar perspective and your brain will do less filtering. This applies not just to finding the mayo, but any difficulty with visual input. For example, if you are having trouble understanding an email, print it out and read it on paper instead of on the screen.[13]

In summary, we wouldn't be nearly as efficient without our mental shortcuts. Paying attention to every little thing all the time wouldn't merely be exhausting, but it would so bombard us with extraneous information that we'd end up paralyzed from information overload.

Nonetheless, many of us filter too much of our lives through shortcuts and past expectations instead of seeing the world clearly. So we should try to go into any situation with both our minds and eyes wide open, seeking different perspectives, so we can experience what's truly happening in the moment—and so we can fully appreciate sudden encounters with the new and amazing.

3. Subconscious Assistance

Our minds have an autopilot much more suited for some tasks than our conscious mind.

Close your eyes and imagine driving down the road and making a lane change, one lane to the right. Take your time and go through the actual motions.

Easily done, right?

If you are like most people you held the wheel straight, then turned it slightly right for a moment, and then straightened it back out. Simple.

The problem is, if you did the exercise the way most people do, you piloted a course right off the road onto the sidewalk!

The correct motion is banking slightly right and then back *through the center* to the left, the same distance you went right, and then finally straightening out.[14] If you don't believe it, go for a drive and test it.

Disconnects between our subconscious mind and our conscious, reasoning mind can be beneficial (such as driving a car without thinking through every move or riding a bicycle or just plain walking). In fact, in sports, athletes undergo significant mental training to let go of conscious step-by-step thoughts. Likewise, musicians couldn't play melodically if they consciously thought about which key to press or which string to fret. They learn to quit thinking and let their subconscious minds take over.

This is wonderful for music or athletics or just everyday living. And, as we discussed in the last chapter, our minds would be overloaded if we had to think consciously about every action.

But this autonomy can also be a problem. Our subconscious minds can drive thoughts leading to poor decisions. The next couple of chapters will explore a few of those influences and suggest ways to overcome them.

4. MERE EXPOSURE

Simple exposure to a concept, object, or person can have a pronounced effect on our opinions, well beyond our conscious thought processing.

Have you ever bought an item only because you were familiar with the brand? Or voted for a candidate only because you were more familiar with the name?

We all have. But just how impressionable are we, and how easily can we be manipulated?

Renowned social psychologist Robert Zajonc wanted to find out. He first contrived a series of nonsense words like *kadirga* or *diliki* and then asked American listeners to guess whether each word meant something good or bad in Turkish. Results: the more often a word was repeated, the more likely the listener guessed a positive meaning.

Then Zajonc tried a similar experiment, this time visual. He projected twenty irregular octagonal shapes onto a dimly lit screen for only a single millisecond, fast enough so viewers could not make out the shape, or any image at all. Then he showed a second series of images with two shapes, a new one, and one from the previous deck. This time each slide was visible for a full second. He then asked which one the viewer liked better. Participants overwhelmingly chose from the first series—even though it was almost indistinguishable to the naked eye.

Why?

Consider evolution. Our brains had to evolve to pay most attention to something novel—good or bad. If we had exposure to something over and over and it didn't bite or hurt us, we became more comfortable with it. And with comfort came a more positive attitude toward it.

Zajonc called this the "mere-exposure effect,"[15] and it's an example of how our likes, dislikes, and choices are not totally conscious. They are often influenced by our hardwired, biased brain in combination with experiences.

Advertisers know this, so we hear brand names over and over. Likewise, publicity, even bad, is a major advantage in politics. Consider the 2016 presidential election. Then-candidate Donald Trump expended great effort to make the news every day. Even though it was not always good news, it kept his name in front of people. It worked.

So, at decision time, we need to take a step back and carefully think through our reasons and consider whether mere exposure is unduly influencing our thought process. The off-brand jeans may be just as good as the Levi's. Or maybe the candidate with the familiar name isn't the most qualified. We need to be aware of all this "noise" in our exposures and take a step back and think with the reasoning part of our minds.

5. RECENCY BIAS

Though it's common knowledge we better remember the most recent things, we seldom realize how this tendency cripples our decisions.

The concept of recency bias is related to the pattern problems and mere exposure issues we discussed above. We instinctively know about recency. It's easiest to recall the last number on a list or the last thing our colleague said. Psychologists have proven this myriad times. That's why salespeople ask to be the last presenter.

But this recency tendency spills over into our decision-making process in a way that may not be beneficial.

We are more likely to estimate probabilities on a "handful of the *latest* outcomes," as opposed to more appropriate long-term data.[16] Jason Zweig, author of *Your Money and Your Brain*, tells us,

"A survey of forecasts by hundreds of individual investors found their expectations of stock returns over the next six months were more than twice as dependent on what the stock market did last week than what it did over the previous few months."[17]

Additionally, we assign the *probability* of an outcome by the ease with which we can call it to mind—and the more recent, the easier it is to recall.[18]

Pair recency and ease of recollection with our pattern recognition faults, and we see why investors fall into reasoning traps. From pattern recognition, we think if a stock has gone up each of the last two or three days, it will probably keep going up.

And the recency bias makes us focus on the most recent, and not the best horizon for analysis. Much better data exists. For example, Fidelity Investments recommends analyzing security performance over various horizons such as tactical (one to twelve months), business cycle (one to ten years), and secular (ten to thirty years).

In summary, it's difficult to escape these faulty influences and it may take significantly more work to overcome them. But the effort should yield much better results over the long term. When it comes to investments or other decisions, business or personal, we must remember the recent trend is no substitute for careful analyses—statistical or other.

6. CONFIRMATION BIAS

We naturally want to be right. And we'll go to great lengths to prove we are, sometimes at the expense of truth.

D o you ever search for information to prove yourself wrong? Likely not often.

We all want to be right, so we seek information to confirm our opinions. We search for support rather than seeking information that could contradict us.

This is especially relevant in the political arena. Conservatives are more likely to watch Fox News, while liberals are more likely to watch MSNBC. Before cable TV, news broadcasters took pride in an unbiased delivery of news. But in an age of instant information, and *lots* of it, many media outlets have evolved (or devolved) to presenting an unabashed slant on the news. Now that we have choices, we seek the channels that agree with us.

But is this really in our best interest?

For our own growth and those around us we need to check out both sides. And we can try getting news from a more neutral source. It's critical for the education of our electorate, the maintenance of a healthy democracy, and our own personal welfare.

It isn't just politics. You may have an opinion on the best way to _____ (insert any topic you want in here), and you'll most likely find someone to confirm it. Just remember, in Columbus's time it was easy to find people to "confirm" the world was flat.

The herd instinct is a product of the confirmation bias. We seek our confirmation in the common behavior of others.

Advertisers use this extensively as they convince us "everyone is doing it," commonly known as the "bandwagon" approach. We all recognize it. Who's mom didn't say, "Just because everyone else is jumping over the cliff doesn't mean you should, too!" But it's hard to escape. To join the crowd is part of our genetic make-up.

The solution is to be aware. Since we are all human beings, we will most likely have the same bias as the crowd, positive or negative. Your mom was right when she told you, "Think for yourself." Beware the herd.

7. HINDSIGHT AND PRECISION BIAS

Not only do we want to be right, we want to be precisely right at the risk of becoming wrong. And we tend to remember getting things right even when we didn't.

Can you think of a time when you correctly predicted an outcome? Did you think, "I just knew it?" Or, "Nailed it?" Maybe you did ... or ... maybe not. Scientists have identified a quirk called hindsight bias. It's a tendency to look back on your prior thoughts or predictions and think you correctly forecasted an event or outcome.

A study was done in 1972 when President Richard Nixon went to China, the first visit by a U.S. president since China turned communist. No one knew what would happen, and the trip was thought a considerable risk. But the trip yielded significant successes for both countries with a pledge to normalize relations.

Just before the trip, dozens of Israeli university students were asked to predict the probability of success. Afterwards, the students were queried about the accuracy of their predictions. Less than two weeks after the trip, 71 percent remembered foretelling a higher probability of success than their documented prediction. Four months after the trip, 81 percent claimed a higher accuracy rate than their actual prediction.[19]

So before we proclaim our visionary prowess, we need to consider the hindsight bias. If we really want to know if we or others are clairvoyant, jotting down the forecast is the only sure proof.

This imperative to be right comes with another quirk. We also aspire to be *precisely* right.

Franck Schuurman, consultant for Decision Strategies International, runs a simple exercise in his lectures. He asks questions like, "In what year was Mozart born?," with a challenge to have 90 percent confidence the correct answer will fall in a chosen range. Respondents could narrowly guess 1730 to 1770, or more broadly, 1600 to 1900. Interestingly, the majority get only five of ten questions correct because they use too a narrow range.[20] They could easily pick a broader range with much higher probability of success. But they insist on precision—or being "more correct."

Unnecessary precision can affect decisions and make you wrong more than you wish. There's nothing wrong with going for a tolerable range if it suits the purpose.

Perhaps that's why your cable TV company tells you their tech will be there sometime between 8:00 a.m. and 5:00 p.m.? Maybe they forgot the "tolerable" part.

8. GREAT EXPECTATIONS

Our expectations can be influenced by things totally unrelated to the object of assessment.

Read the following description of a person called Jim:
Jim is intelligent, skillful, industrious, warm, determined, practical, and cautious. Mark the one trait in each pair that most likely represents Jim:

Generous-------Not Generous
Unhappy--------Happy
Irritable----------Good-natured
Humorous-------Humorless

Seventy-five to 95 percent of people think Jim is generous, happy, good natured, and humorous. However, when the word *warm* is changed to *cold*, only 5 to 35 percent think Jim will have these traits.[21]

We think if a person has good qualities in one area, he or she will have good qualities in other areas. Scientists call this the "the halo effect."

Human resource managers will admit that better-looking people have an edge in getting hired. Likewise, people who perform well in their operative job are often thought better prospects for management, despite not necessarily displaying management skills.

These positive associations extend beyond observable characteristics to other sensory experiences.

Experiment participants were handed either a warm cup of coffee or a cold drink from a complete stranger. Those receiving the warm coffee were more likely to consider the stranger to be a "warm person."[22]

Our subconscious expectations influence us even though we know they should not.

However, these expectations can be used to our benefit.

A study analyzed patients recovering from abdominal surgery. One group was told what to expect, such as how long the pain would last, what type of pain they would experience, and when they would regain consciousness. The other group was told nothing. Patients who were told what to expect experienced less pain, required less medication, and recovered earlier than those who were told nothing.

In summary, expectations are a powerful influence, driven not only by hardwired subconscious predispositions like the "halo effect" but also by our conscious expectations. We need to be aware of this influence and carefully reason through our perceptions. But the good news is expectations can also be used in a positive manner as we'll discuss further in several chapters in Part Two.

9. THE SUNK COST FALLACY

Our minds can easily deceive us when it comes to matters of relative costs and benefits.

I magine you arrived at your local movie theater, reached into your pocket for the twenty-dollar general admission ticket you purchased an hour ago, and discovered that you'd lost it. Would you buy another ticket?

Alternatively, imagine that you didn't purchase anything in advance, but when arriving at the theater, you reached into your pocket and realized that you'd lost the twenty-dollar bill you were planning to use for admission. Would you still buy the ticket?

Princeton University psychologists Daniel Kahneman and Amos Tversky ran these two scenarios by test subjects back in 1984 (albeit with cheaper tickets; I've adjusted for inflation).

As it turned out, 88 percent of those who imagined losing the twenty-dollar bill said they'd go ahead and buy the ticket.

But only 46 percent of those who imagined losing the ticket said they'd buy a replacement ticket.[23]

Why the difference?

Financially, the same thing happened across the board—everyone lost twenty dollars.

But those who imagined losing the twenty-dollar bill didn't attach that loss to the ticket. They therefore had little reason to not simply fish out another twenty dollars and see the movie as planned. In other words, they mentally wrote off the loss, forgot about it, and moved on with their lives.

In contrast, the second group was dealing with the pain of not only losing money, but of taking the risk of exchanging something they possessed—the twenty-dollar bill—for something they didn't—the movie ticket—and having it turn out badly. On an emotional level they probably weren't even aware of, they didn't want to immediately take a similar risk that might make them feel even worse (e.g., "What if I paid another twenty dollars, for a total of forty dollars, and it turned out the movie sucked?").

At the same time, not buying another ticket mitigated the pain by letting them tell themselves they hadn't lost anything beyond what they'd already planned—because they'd intended to spend twenty dollars, and that's what ended up happening.

However, all of that is irrational. The truth is the first and second tickets actually have nothing to do with each other. Seeing the movie was worth twenty dollars when the first ticket was purchased, and the movie hadn't changed an hour later, so it continued to be worth twenty dollars; and that's the only factor worth considering if looked at unemotionally.

While the stakes were relatively low in this scenario—not seeing a movie—the tendency to care more about what we've lost, or what we're at risk of losing, than what we can gain is actually hardwired into our brains. In the past, it had genuine value for our survival. But in our modern era dominated by continual change, this way of thinking—sometimes referred to as the "sunk cost fallacy"—can be a major handicap.

For example, those who play the stock market should base their decisions to sell or buy based solely on the most current and accurate information available to them. However, many people keep in mind what they paid for a stock, and will hold onto even a clear loser as it keeps falling lower and lower in the hope that it somehow goes back up again to at least the price they originally paid—because they want to avoid the emotional pain of admitting to a choice that turned out badly and of feeling, even for a moment, like a failure.

Investors have lost millions of dollars this way.

There are also many instances of the sunk cost fallacy in business. For example, Kodak dominated the photography market from the 1900s through the 1970s, but it made most of its profits from selling film, and its leaders wouldn't emotionally accept the industry's switch to film-less digital photography—even though one of its own employees invented the first digital camera in 1975! Had Kodak adapted to the times, it could've become a major player in smart phone cameras, or another Facebook or Instagram. But by refusing to let go of its past investments in film, Kodak grew disconnected from its customers, and the company has now all but disappeared.

You may be able to think of sunk cost fallacy experiences in your own life—for example, dating someone who wasn't really the right fit, or hanging onto a stressful job, for a lot longer than was good for you.

If so, you were only being human.

The old saying "A bird in the hand is worth two in the bush" reflects this mentality. While it might at first sound like common sense, the sunk cost fallacy is telling you to value what you already possess over what you have the potential to achieve.

Instead, you should take a close look at what you're holding onto, and consider whether you might be better off letting it go— to free your hands to receive something of far greater value.

10. ATTRIBUTING VALUE

When our mind is assigning value it can be tricked rather easily.

The sunk cost fallacy is one quirk in how we perceive value. Are there others?

Imagine you are in morning rush hour at the main subway station in Washington, D.C. An ordinary man dressed in jeans and a baseball cap takes out his violin and performs with extraordinary ability. He plays some of the most difficult pieces ever written for violin. What would you think? An incredibly talented street performer?

In 2007 the *Washington Post* sponsored an undercover field story that created the scenario above. During the forty-three-minute concert, there was no thunderous applause and no cameras flashing. In fact, of the 1,097 people who walked by, hardly anyone stopped to listen.

No one knew at the time, but the man in the baseball cap was Joshua Bell, one of the finest violinists alive, a regular performer to *sold-out* crowds in the most prestigious concert halls. And his violin was a $3,500,000 Stradivarius. But since he wasn't dressed in formal attire, and there was no stage, Mr. Bell looked like an ordinary street performer and passersby saw and heard only an ordinary street musician.[24]

To be fair, many distractions played into the subway experiment. Commuters were rushing to work, and the acoustics and noisiness of the environment weren't conducive to a good concert experience.

But what if an experiment were designed with just one variable: price?

Dan Ariely, a professor of psychology and behavior economics at Duke University, set up such an experiment using SoBe

Adrenaline Rush, a beverage claiming to increase mental acuity. He developed a thirty-minute word jumble to assess the effects of the drink related to price and administered it to three different groups of students.

One group was told about the intelligence-enhancing properties and asked to watch a video while allowing time for the drink to take effect. They were also required to sign an authorization allowing researchers to charge their university account $2.89.

A second group was given the drink, the story, and video, but were told the university got a discount, and were only charged eighty-nine cents for the drink.

A third group, the control group, took the test without drinking SoBe or watching the video.

The results were interesting. The group charged $2.89 for the drink did, in fact, do slightly better than the control group. But the group who drank the "cheaper" SoBe performed *significantly worse* than the control group!

Ariely's summation was this: "The intriguing idea is that expectations change the reality we live in. When you get something at a discount, the positive expectations don't kick in as strongly."

But what if it's free? Are expectations the same? Next chapter.

II. THE VALUE OF FREE

Our minds confuse "free" and real value.

In an earlier chapter we found we're hardwired to avoid loss, and so value what we have over what we can potentially gain. In the last chapter, we learned our expectations can also cause errant value judgments.

An interesting off-shoot of these phenomena is our love affair with things that are free.

In his bestselling book *Predictably Irrational,* Dan Ariely relates an experiment he conducted with chocolate. Ariely set up a table in a large public building to sell two items: a Hershey's Kiss for a penny or a Lindt truffle for fifteen cents. (Dated prices based on the time of the experiment.) Customers were allowed to buy only one piece of chocolate, so they had to choose between the two offerings.

A Hershey's Kiss normally costs around six cents, so one cent was an excellent price.

And a Lindt truffle, which is a significantly higher quality of chocolate, normally costs around thirty-five cents, so fifteen cents was an even better price.

The clear bargain was the Lindt truffle, which offered a discount of around twenty cents vs. the Hershey's Kiss being discounted for around five cents; plus, the truffle tasted way better.

And that was borne out by sales. A whopping 73 percent of customers bought the Lindt truffle.

Then Ariely lowered the price of both chocolates by a penny. As a result, the Lindt truffle became fourteen cents, and the Hershey's Kiss became free.

While a one cent change might seem trivial, it made a world of difference. The free Hershey's Kiss won over 69 percent of the customers, a result nearly opposite of the previous one—even though the Lindt truffle remained a greater bargain and tastier choice.

To make sure this wasn't an aberration, Ariely ran several variants of the experience (changing the types of chocolates, eliminating anyone's need to have spare change, etc.). They all ended up with the same result.

Why did the switch to free make such a powerful difference?

Because, as a previous chapter explained, we're wired to be wary of giving up what we have for what we can obtain. And when we make a choice that doesn't end well, we're wired to feel awful about it.

When something is free, though, it bypasses that entire mental mechanism. If we're paying nothing, then we don't have to worry about potential loss, because we're not giving up anything we own or putting anything at risk.

In other words, a free item literally frees us to act without our usual mental baggage.

That's why so many companies offer products for free to get you involved as a customer. They know it's a big hurdle to convince you to buy something you've never tried before, because you're nervous about not liking it and then having to deal with a feeling of loss. But if you try a product for free, you can avoid both financial and emotional risk—and have the chance of deciding you really do like the product and want to make it a part of your life.

That said, Ariely's chocolate experiment also demonstrates the downside of choosing free things. When you choose something that costs you nothing over something that's actually better for you, you're cheating yourself of a superior experience.

For example, if you stay home to watch TV to enjoy something you truly love, such as an amazing drama or comedy series, or the day's news, that's great. But if you're watching TV only because it's free—or because you've already paid for it—then you should consider going out more to experience live events and interact with new people. It'll cost money, but it'll be worth it for the new experiences and relationships you gain.

So "free" is wonderful if it eases us into trying something new that might merit our time and attention. But we should beware of reflexively choosing something free over something that's likely to provide us with a richer, fuller life.

12. THE REALITY OF MONEY

We value real money differently than equivalent cash substitutes such as credit cards or cash replacements, sometimes leading us into irresponsible actions.

To demonstrate this, Dan Ariely (as noted before) conducted studies with MIT and Harvard students in which participants were told to solve as many math problems as they could in five minutes. One group was told to submit their sheets and they would get paid 50 cents for each correct answer. A second group was told to tear up their answer sheets and simply tell the experimenter their score in exchange for payment, making it possible to cheat. The third was told was told the same as the second, except rather than cash, they would receive a token for each right answer that they could then exchange for cash just twelve feet across the room

Guess what? The participants who received tokens lied much more than those who were paid directly in physical cash. The honest group solved an average of 3.5 correctly. The tear-up-the-sheet-and-get-cash-group reported 6.2 correct questions. But the "tear up sheet and get tokens" group proffered a whopping 9.4 questions "solved."

In other words, those working with cash substitutes were much more willing to indulge in self-deceit and rationalization.[25] Ariely says it's much easier to be dishonest when we are one step removed from cash. And that includes deceiving ourselves.

The ramifications of this experiment become apparent when considering credit cards. We're likely to spend more quickly, in larger amounts, and with less pain when paying with plastic than with cash. (In fact, numerous subsequent studies have confirmed this.)

So if you find yourself perpetually running low on funds, consider paying more often with hard cash.

Alternatively, if you're buying online, try picturing yourself paying the amount with a one-, five-, ten-, or twenty-dollar bill before you click to approve the purchase.

Another helpful practice is to pay each credit card bill as soon as it comes in. This trains your mind to recognize that those intangible numbers end up translating at the end of the month into real money.

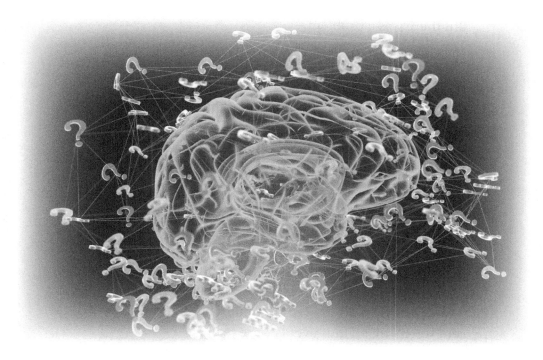

13. Reliability of Memory

Memories are reconstructed every time we recall them. In the process we tend to distort them, sometimes to a great extent, even recalling false memories.

It turns out our personal memories aren't nearly as reliable as we think. It doesn't mean memories are useless, but we need to understand a few alarming principles, principles that affect our actions and decisions.

In 1992 a cargo plane crashed into an Amsterdam apartment building. Less than a year later, 55 percent of the Dutch population recalled watching TV and seeing the plane hit the building, with many able to recall specifics such as the angle of descent or whether the plane was on fire before crashing.

But there was a problem.

The event was never caught on video! The mass recollection had been pieced together from descriptions and pictures of the event.[26]

Our memories are made from bits and scraps reconstructed whenever a recollection takes place. That means each recollection from the past may trigger the addition of new details, shading of the facts, or even pruning of a few key facts. And we don't realize we're doing so.[27]

It's not difficult to implant a false memory. Psychologist Elizabeth Loftus at the University of Washington conducted an experiment during which she gave volunteers a booklet narrating three true stories from each volunteer's childhood plus an added false story describing being lost in the mall at age five. When asked later to write down all they could remember about the events, 25 percent were sure all four events were real![28]

Other cognitive scientists have provided evidence that false memory is a normal occurrence. One study observed that adult twins often disagree about which one experienced an event in childhood. For example, they might differ in their recollection of which twin, at age eight, was pushed off the bike by the neighbor. Even the most basic information like who was involved can get "rearranged."[29]

For more information on this fascinating topic, search for Elizbeth Loftus as noted above. She's done extensive work on memory issues.

So the next time we argue with our spouse or friend over what happened ten years ago, we may want to consult books, documents, yearbooks, the Web (maybe, as we'll discuss later) or something more reliable than our memory.

Likewise, we shouldn't start thinking we are getting senile when we lose the argument about what happened. We're just being human, again!

14. Efficiency Deficiency

Our brain will devote little energy to storing information it can easily access externally.

Before we become too critical of our poor overworked brain, we need to give it credit for fuel-efficiency in allocating resources. Scientists believe our brain evolved to use as little energy as possible. Back in the early days, our species didn't know when the next meal was coming. An energy-efficient brain was an evolutionary advantage that remains today despite our ready availability of brain fuel. As noted in pattern discussion, our brains would quickly become overloaded if we processed every detail. So evolution and necessity has taught our brains to work only as hard as necessary. And our brain may do that without us consciously knowing it.

As an example, today we have the Google phenomenon. If we hear or read a fact, and we know we can easily look it up on Google, our brain will expend little or no effort trying to memorize it.[30] We go into power-saving mode. All we remember is what is required to find the fact again. In this case, a few touches or clicks of the mouse.

We can avoid this quirk by giving cues to our brain to switch on memory. As an example, we could envision needing to know first aid or the location of a hospital during a medical emergency, where no phone signal is available.

Gord Hotchkiss, past chairman of the Search Marketing Professionals Association (and an expert in online user behavior), thinks this same power-saving principle is at work in communications.

According to Hotchkiss, "Face-to-face communication can put a huge cognitive load on our brains. We're receiving communication on a much greater bandwidth than with text. When we're across from a person, we not only hear what they're saying, we're reading emotional cues, watching facial expression, interpreting body language, and monitoring vocal tones."[31] So it's no surprise that texting is becoming the communication mode of choice for many people. It's less cognitive load.

As we all know, the course of least resistance is not always the best. At the extreme level it's not good practice to propose to the future bride by text. Likewise, that conversation with the boss about performance and a potential raise, warrants all the cognitive resources we can muster. We can all think of many more examples along the continuum.

So maybe there is a good reason for that next meeting we were dreading to attend?

15. RELYING ON THE PAST

We tend to over-rely on the past as an indicator of the future, even when we know conditions in the future are different.

Imagine you are in the class of Professor J. Keith Murnighan of Northwestern University. He's running an exercise for his MBA students where he auctions off a real twenty-dollar bill with simple, but strongly stated, rules.[32]

1. Bidding proceeds in dollar increments and the highest bidder gets the twenty-dollar bill.

2. The second highest bidder also pays what he or she bid and *gets nothing*.

3. It *is* for real money.

So are you willing to pay a dollar or two or all the way up to nineteen dollars for a twenty?

Murnighan notes it's easy to get the bidding going. Many students set limits for themselves as they have in prior auctions. But, the rules in this auction soon make that thinking irrelevant. Not surprisingly, after the bidding reaches twenty dollars, most everyone drops out except the last two bidders. If you find yourself in second place, you'll pay anyway, so why not bid another two dollars to avoid paying nineteen dollars for nothing? The problem is deciding when to stop and accept that other bidders will think the same and send you on an endless journey like mice on a wheel.

It's not unusual for the "winner" to pay fifty dollars for the auctioned twenty-dollar bill and the loser to pay forty-nine dollars for nothing. In one case, the loser paid in excess of one hundred dollars! Remember, according to the rules, the loser pays his last bid too. So there is motivation to keep bidding to win twenty dollars to partially offset your losses.

The emotional components of this exercise clouded decision-making, as we'll discuss later. But the students' historical familiarity with the auction process misled them into major pitfalls. Though they heard the rule about second place paying, they weren't deterred. Murnighan often does a second auction right after the first and students fall into the same trap.

Reasoning through pitfalls is not easy when our historical reference point is strong. When emotions take over, and we realize we are in over our head, we will find it difficult to think rationally. Though the students understood the rules, something in their brain latched on to prior auction experience rather than looking forward and analyzing potential consequences.

Business research has determined that companies often make decisions based on past occurrences, without evaluating current trends in customer behavior, market, or environmental conditions.

Almost half of the twenty-five exemplar companies in Tom Peters and Robert Waterman's 1982 book, *In Search of Excellence,* are no longer in business. Likewise, of the original S&P 500 list created in 1957, only 15 percent are still on the list today. Many of these companies failed because they became overconfident that past successful strategies would work again in the future.[33]

So when we make our decisions, it's important to examine our scaffold or framework that evolved from our past experiences, and then consider new information that could, and should, change our understanding.

So how much information do we need? Next chapter.

16. Information Overload

Information overload is real. Our brain can only process limited amounts of data.

When was the last time you checked Google for decision information? Likely recently. Why not? It's the ultimate knowledge base. With Google we get as much information and as many (emphasis on "*as many*") comparisons as we choose.

Are we making better decisions? Scientists say maybe not.

In fact, research in decision science shows people faced with too many choices are likely to make no decision at all.

Sheena Ivengar at Columbia University studied participation in business 401(k) programs and found participation declined from 75 to 70 percent when the choices went from 2 to 11. Participation further dropped to just 61 percent when the options went to 59.[34] (If you are unfamiliar with 401(k) programs, the incentive is significant: not enrolling in a 401(k) is like throwing money away. Employers typically match a percentage of employees' contributions.) This is a simple example of information overload. Other studies in more impactful areas, such as air traffic and medicine, reveal the same result. The bottom line is, we can only process so much information.

So how do we deal with information overload?

In earlier chapters we discussed ways to override information from our subconscious brain. But it has a purpose, and this is one of them. Researchers have found creative decisions are more likely to bubble up from a brain applying unconscious thought as opposed to a full-frontal analytical assault."[35] A decision requiring assessment of complex information is not best approached by methodical and conscious means. Results may be better and regrets fewer if we give our subconscious mind time to process the info and remove ourselves from the inflow. The adage, "sleep on it," has merit.

We should set our priorities, too. If the decision hinges on a few criteria, we should concentrate on those and not get bogged down by irrelevant data. Some people naturally do this. Take TV channel surfers. The "deciders" just find an acceptable program and stop. The "maximizers," search endlessly, absorbing all kinds of information and struggling with a decision.[36]

So, are you a decider or a maximizer? We need to learn to be deciders if a decision is required and hinges on a few criteria. Maximizers have their place, though. Sometimes a decision is secondary to seeking new experiences, like searching for a vacation destination or looking for a new book to read.

17. EMOTIONS AND RISK

Emotions can have an over-sized impact on our risk assessments.

In a simple experiment, volunteers were told to imagine being called to the doctor's office for an urgent medical matter. Another group was not burdened with imagining such a stressful event. Both groups were then asked to pick between a relatively safe 60 percent chance of winning five dollars or a riskier 30 percent chance of winning ten dollars. The anxiety-induced people were much more likely to take the safe bet.[37] This simple experiment illustrates how we fail to understand that our emotional response from one event can affect our ability to make decisions regarding an unrelated event.

The anxiety factor can be even more complex. In another study, men were asked to think of either three or eight factors increasing their chances of heart disease. Those who named only three factors rated their overall risk of heart disease higher than those who were forced to think of eight.

Experimenters concluded that men forced to think of eight had to work much harder. (Try coming up with eight yourself!) They subconsciously thought, *If it's that hard to think of eight reasons, my risk must not be that great!* Conversely, those who had to think of only three found the short list easier to recall, making the risk seem more real.[38] Herein we find a serious problem with assessing risk: *the easier to call to mind, the more real the risk seems.*

This "ease to call to mind" is influenced by other factors.

"Recency," as discussed earlier, is one.

But even more powerful is how vivid the event seems. For example, people pay twice as much for hospitalization insurance for a specific disease than for a policy that covers any medical issue. "Any issue" is vague but "cancer" is vivid.[39]

Likewise, people fear an attack, clear the beach, and even stay away from the ocean altogether at the slightest mention of, "Shark!"

But the odds of being killed in a shark attack are 1 in 3,943,110! Compare that to the odds of dying in a motor vehicle accident: 1 in 88! But we don't think twice about climbing into our cars every day. Thanks to movies like *Jaws* we can envision those ferocious shark teeth. We can easily recall the image and trigger an anxious response, coloring our perception of probability.

Even an alarming word or phrase can factor into our anxiety response.

Elizabeth Loftus conducted an experiment where participants were shown videos of car accidents. Some were asked how fast the cars were going when they "hit each other." Others were asked how fast they were going when they "smashed into each other." Both groups were shown the same videos, but the ones prompted by the words "smashed into" estimated the speed 19 percent faster.[40] "Smashed" is more vivid than "hit."

Part of the solution is simply to be aware.

We can mitigate the recency issue by putting time in between an event and our decision. But the vivid images issue is difficult to overcome. Many people are still much more anxious about flying than driving despite flying being safer. We must keep telling ourselves that the statistics are true and try to recruit that reasoning part of our brain.

18. Stories

We prefer stories as opposed to good data to support our decisions, sometimes resulting in sub-optimal actions.

Imagine you are considering buying a new car and check *Consumer Reports* to find a highly reliable choice. But then you go to a party and find a friend bought the very same vehicle and complains he takes it to the repair shop often. He says, "nothing but trouble."

Will you buy that car?

If you're like most people, you won't. The account from your friend will have more bearing on your decision than the statistics. But should it? Your friend is a sample of one, while the *Consumer Reports* data are based on large numbers of vehicles. There is variance in everything, and even the best-made cars have an occasional "lemon." It could be that your friend got one of these rare lemons, or maybe he or she hasn't kept up with the recommended maintenance.

The point is, by not buying the car you'd be basing your decision on one person's narrative, not reliable statistical data.[41] But excluding the story from your decision is difficult.

Our fondness for stories is hardwired in us. In the history of humankind, only recently have we been able to record and store accessible facts for the knowledge we need. Prior to such capabilities, we passed our history and knowledge from generation to generation by telling stories.

We all love a good story. We have an evolved penchant for paying close attention to them.[42] But, our preference for stories or anecdotal evidence over facts and figures can be a problem. It intertwines with our "ease to call to mind" issue. Stories are much easier to remember than statistics.

This tendency is not lost on politicians. In recent elections "toughening up on crime" was brought up frequently. We hear story after story of violent crimes and get the impression crime is running rampant. Our media feeds us a steady diet of gruesome news. News outlets have the motto "If it bleeds, it leads." Such reporting tricks us into feeling the world is becoming more dangerous. Campaigning politicians capitalize on this fear and run on platforms dedicated to beefing up police forces and cracking down on gang violence. They share the tragic and/or scary stories of crime victims. No one could argue that these incidents are not problematic, and we would all agree we should do more. But we need perspective in decisions on policy.

The truth is violent crime in the U.S. was down by 51 percent between 1993 and 2018, the most recent data available. Likewise, property crime was down 54 percent over the same period.[43] Note the graphs below courtesy of the Pew Research Center, Washington, D.C., October 17, 2019.

Crime rates have fallen since the early 1990s

Trends in U.S. violent crime and property crime, 1993-2018

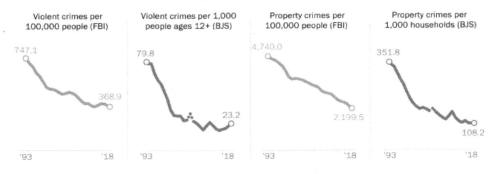

Violent crimes per 100,000 people (FBI)	Violent crimes per 1,000 people ages 12+ (BJS)	Property crimes per 100,000 people (FBI)	Property crimes per 1,000 households (BJS)
747.1 → 368.9	79.8 → 23.2	4,740.0 → 2,199.5	351.8 → 108.2

Note: FBI figures include reported crimes only. Bureau of Justice Statistics (BJS) figures include unreported and reported crimes. 2006 BJS estimates are not comparable to those in other years due to methodological changes.
Source: FBI, Bureau of Justice Statistics.

PEW RESEARCH CENTER

So, despite the nightly news, the country is not "going to hell in a handbasket." But politicians know we believe and relate to stories. They will rely on anecdotal evidence to raise anxiety levels and garner votes.

We can't blame politicians for using stories. It is effective. But we all must realize the stories we're hearing in the news give us a false impression. Case in point, the subject of school shootings has significantly raised anxiety for both parents and students. Rightly so, given the headlines. But according to author James Alan Fox of *The Wiley Handbook on Violence in Education, 2018,* "There is not an epidemic of school shootings."

In his book, Fox notes that there were four times as many children shot and killed in schools in the early 1990s compared with more recent statistics. In fact, more children are killed every year drowning in pools or in bicycle accidents than in school shootings. Fox is quick to point out that this doesn't mean we should ignore the problem, but policy-makers need to base decisions on facts, allowing for a reasoned response that doesn't unnecessarily scare people or infringe on civil liberties.[44] Overly militarizing schools with armed guards or educators may only add to anxiety.

The same concept applies internationally. Our daily diet of journalism would have us believe the world is getting more violent every day. But it isn't, even considering terrorist attacks. According to Nigel Barber, PhD, "The worldwide probability of dying in a terrorist attack is infinitesimal, at less than one in a million per year. The risk is three times lower than in the 1980s. Yet, survey respondents believe the risk has increased."[45] We compound this misconception by factoring fear into everyday decisions—for example, choosing to drive rather than fly, due to the possibility of a terror attack. But doing so actually increases risk, because flying is statistically much safer than driving.[46]

Steven Pinker, Harvard psychologist, studied this topic in depth, and has shown that past decades had much more violence than the present. During World War II, three hundred of every one hundred thousand people each year were lost to war. During the Korean War it was twenty people per one hundred thousand. It then dropped to the teens during the Vietnam War and then fell to the single digits per one hundred thousand people. In the twenty-first century it's been below one war death per one hundred thousand people per year.[47]

This is not to imply that any level of violence is acceptable, but the world is making progress, despite all the news coverage. Violence has actually decreased and is less pervasive than at any time in history. The reason? According to Pinker, it's because we are getting smarter.

Pinker's studies of IQ tests show the average teenager is smarter with each generation. IQ test scores are adjusted over time, so 100 remains average. But if you were to keep the test the same, a teenager who scores 100 today would have scored 118 in 1950 and 130 in 1910. This year's average kid would have been a near genius in 1910, and generally, with increased intelligence comes an increased adversity to violence. We find more advanced ways to "turn swords into plowshares."[48] And we need to use these smarts for more than turning away from violence. We need to fight this human desire for stories, especially gruesome ones, and our media's incessant coverage of negative events. How often have we seen good news headlines?

Likely, rarely. We need to understand that news covers what happened. It doesn't cover what didn't happen. That we have fewer violent crimes seldom makes the news, and the number of tragic stories far outweighs "good" news.

We also need to recognize that we are hearing and seeing more news than ever before. Events happening all over our world are brought to our attention daily. Twenty-four-hour news coverage is available in the palm of our hand. We need to avoid the barrage of negativity and maybe even decrease time spent watching or reading the news. Once a day is plenty.

A third strategy is more introspective. We need to pay attention to the ideas forming in our minds and question them. In the words of Euripides over 2,400 years ago, "Man's most valuable trait is a judicious sense of what not to believe." Seeking the truth through statistics is more important than ever. Let's not get caught up in the stories. In a nutshell, *we need to learn to live statistically*.

RECOMMENDED READING FOR PART ONE

---

1. *Your Money and Your Brain: How the New Science of Neuroeconomics Can Help Make You Rich* by Jason Zweig

2. *Don't Believe Everything You Think: The 6 Basic Mistakes We Make In Thinking* by Thomas E. Kida

3. *Predictably Irrational: The Hidden Forces That Shape Our Decisions* by Dan Ariely

4. *Sway: The Irresistible Pull of Irrational Behavior* by Ori Brafman and Rom Brafman

PART TWO

How Our Brain Changes

"Observe constantly that all things take place by change, and accustom thyself to consider that the nature of the Universe loves nothing so much as to change the things which are, and to make new things like them."

—Marcus Aurelius

19. NEUROPLASTICITY

Neuroplasticity is a big word driving big excitement. It refers to the brain's ability to change its own structure in ways before thought impossible.

A true-life example will help.

For a few dark moments, imagine your three-year-old granddaughter was in a tragic accident. You're told by physicians that your granddaughter—we'll call her Lorie—has sustained severe brain damage and they're even recommending transferring her to a facility where she can pass in peace.

The damage is extensive. Many of the connections between the two hemispheres of Lorie's brain were either severed or severely damaged. But you notice something the doctors do not. When you look into her eyes, she seems to smile.

This really happened. Grandparents Cal and Janet (names changed) faced this frightful dilemma.

They did not give up. The smiles were the way they communicated with Lorie for months.

Janet wheeled Lorie down the hospital hall and Cal played games with her by hiding behind doors and jumping out yelling, "Boo!"—to which Lorie smiled. Yet the doctors still insisted nothing was there.

Fast forward eight years.

I first met Lorie when her grandfather brought her to a birthday party. She was beaming, chatty, articulate, and exuding an energy level only possible for an eleven-year-old. In every way, she seemed a normal energetic pre-adolescent, but more mature, as with the ease with which she chatted with her elders. Lorie brought an aura of sunshine and pleasantness to the room that everyone enjoyed. Her grandfather, Cal, was clearly proud of her.

Cal and Janet had not given up. Through the years they dedicated countless hours and persevered with various therapies and learning exercises based on concepts in succeeding chapters.

To prepare for writing this book, I met with Lorie's grandfather for an update. At this writing Lorie is a sophomore in high school and an athlete. She has swimming trophies and is competing with success at state levels. To look at her you would think *Olympian*. She has a ready wit, ribs her grandfather incessantly, and exudes excitement and sunshine.

Lorie's doctors at a prestigious hospital admit they have never been so happy to have been so wrong. She visits them annually, and tests show Lorie has grown many new connections between the two halves of her brain.

Per grandfather Cal, one of Lorie's favorite pastimes is riding in the family convertible (hoping soon to drive it) and playing Neil Diamond with the sound way up to "teenager" level.

One of her favorite songs is Neal Diamond's "Hell Yeah." If Lorie's story fascinates you, envision her riding off in the convertible singing at the top of her lungs with fist pumps in the air. Then look up the song lyrics. You'll gain a new appreciation for the song.

Growing new brain cells is not entirely unexpected of a young child. But at three years old, Lorie's brain was about 80 percent the size it would be as an adult. Could the final growth—20 percent—of Lorie's brain "fit in" to assist? Lorie's brain was so severely damaged doctors found it difficult to believe. And, back then, scientists believed that current brain cells didn't reproduce.

But Lorie's brain defied all these prior concepts. Lorie's brain pulled off the miracle that is the stuff of neuroplasticity.

So how could her doctors have been so wrong?

Until the end of the twentieth-century, prevailing theories held that, though young children generated new brain cells, the adult human brain was hardwired after early formative years. In other words, upon reaching adulthood, we would develop all the brain cells we would get, and those cells were genetically coded to do certain tasks.

Scientists also knew connections (synapses) between brain cells (neurons) could change and that learning resulted from changing these connections (sprouting dendrites) or strengthening them. The accepted theory of "cells that fire together wire together," drove these concepts. In other words, the neurons that fired together in a chain changed in such a way that made it more likely that firing one would fire the other. Thus, "wired together."

And this was the extent of what scientists thought the brain could do. Now we know differently. Lorie's "neuroplasticity" was well beyond this retail variety of synaptic connection or strengthening. We're talking about wholesale changes previously deemed impossible. The brain is capable of reorganizing itself. The next several chapters discuss these miraculous changes.

BRAIN BUZZED

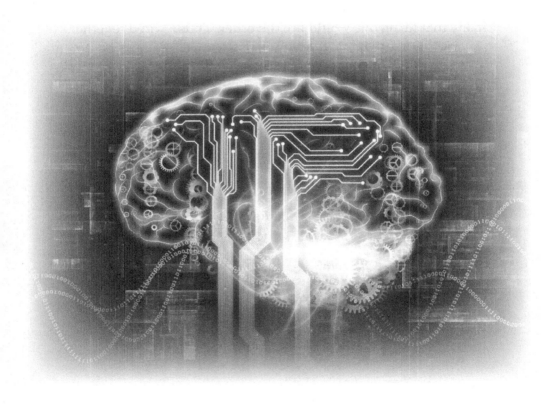

20. THE RACE FOR CORTICAL EXPANSION

Our brain is capable of recruiting additional cortex for important tasks, cortex beyond those areas originally dedicated to certain functions.

Noted neuroscientist Alvaro Pascual-Leone of the Harvard Medical School conducted a deceptively simple experiment. He instructed volunteers to learn a five-finger piano exercise and try to play it as fluidly as possible while keeping up to a metronome's constant sixty beats per minute. They were asked to practice two hours a day, every day, for five days. Then it was test time.

Only this was not the proficiency test to which Harvard medical students were accustomed. Over the course of the five days, subjects underwent "transcranial-magnetic-stimulation" (TMS) testing to infer functions of neurons in specific locations in the brain. Scientists tested every day after practice to map how much of each volunteer's cortex controlled finger movements.

The part of the cortex dedicated to these finger movements expanded and "took over" surrounding areas of the brain "like dandelions on a suburban lawn," a result well beyond just strengthening connections.[49] The brains of these students were recruiting new neurons for the musical task at hand, neurons presumably previously dedicated to other, less-often-used functions. Other studies have confirmed the results—providing proof that greater use of muscles causes more cortex tissue to be devoted to that specific task.

This expansion of recruited cortex was contrary to prior genetic coded disposition theory. But it wasn't difficult to imagine, nor was it especially surprising.

But the next step was.

Pascual-Leone and his team continued the study but added a group that merely *thought* about the piano exercise. They imagined their fingers playing the piano part while keeping their hands still. Results were unexpected, to say the least: Volunteers who *only mentally practiced* recorded similar physical reorganization of their cortex.

Let's restate that.

Volunteers who did *zero* physical rehearsing, and only mentally imagined the practice, had physical reorganization of their cortex similar to participants who practiced physically!

This concept is used extensively today by athletes, musicians, and even people giving speeches. When you can't practice physically, a mental rehearsal can still be of great benefit.

Think of the possibilities. The following chapters explore in more depth.

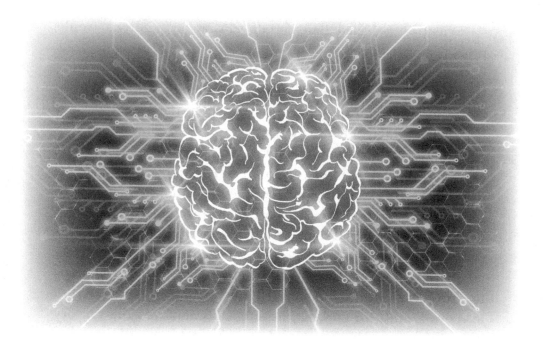

21. CORTICAL REORGANIZATION

Our brain is capable of recruiting additional cortex to replace cortex damaged from stroke or other injury.

The last chapter demonstrated the brain could expand areas designed to handle certain motor functions. But if a limb is severed or suffers nerve damage, what happens to that part of the brain?

Likewise, what happens if part of the brain itself is damaged, as in Lorie's case? Could the brain recruit other areas of the brain to replace damaged tissue?

The old dogma said, "absolutely not." Such thinking lowered therapy expectations for stroke victims and the prospects of fixing pathological wiring responsible for psychiatric disorders.

Scientists believed that certain clusters of neurons would process signals from your nose and other clusters of neurons would process signals from your fingers, and they'd do nothing else until the day you died. If you severed the nerve in your finger, the associated brain cluster should have "gone dark."

Michael Merzenich, PhD, and professor emeritus at the University of California at San Francisco, questioned these theories. In well-intended but controversial research, he severed the finger nerves of laboratory monkeys. Several months afterward, he found the part of the cortex that originally responded to the finger was now responding to signals from other parts of the hand![50]

Likewise, Edward Taub, PhD and behavioral neuroscientist at the University of Alabama at Birmingham, searched for solutions for stroke victims. He wondered if sensory feedback was necessary to move a limb. To find out, he surgically removed the sensory nerve from one or both arms of lab monkeys to stop all sensation from their limb(s). But before the experiment was finished, animal rights activists rescued the monkeys and removed them from the experiment.

However, twelve years later, scientists revisited the project. Several of the monkeys were to be euthanized to spare them further suffering. Aware of the original purpose of the experiment, the scientists persuaded authorities to allow a final examination of the monkeys' brains to determine what happened to the "arm" region of the brain after having no sensation for years.

It wasn't silent. It had changed jobs. It now processed signals from the face instead. And the region now responsible for receiving sensations from the face had grown 10 to 14 square millimeters, in what scientists described as "a massive cortical reorganization."[51]

The same phenomenon has been detected in humans. People blind from birth who become proficient in Braille provide evidence that the visual cortex can switch jobs to process tactile signals from the fingers.

But what about later in life?

Pascual-Leone took the next step. He blindfolded sighted volunteers for five days and had them spend their time learning Braille and sharpening their hearing. Brain scans were conducted before and after, with results confirming theory. When volunteers touched an object or heard sounds, activity in their visual cortex increased—a finding considered impossible by previous thought.[52]

So what could this mean for stroke victims?

Taub had inferred that, if stroke had damaged one area, the brain could recruit another to do the job. But if the brain could do this, why were stroke patients unable to use their affected limbs?

Taub reasoned that, in part, it was because of *learned non-use*: the patients stopped trying to use the affected limb. They had grown used to their disabled limbs and they assumed they could not make improvements.

If this was true, the trick was to *force* patients to use the affected limb. To do so, Taub put the "good" arm of his patients in a sling, forcing stroke sufferers to use their affected arm. And force them he did, with a whole regimen of exercises performed for 90 percent of waking hours over ten straight days. After this short but intensive rehab period, Taub found patients regained significant use of an arm they thought would dangle uselessly for the rest of their life.[53]

Taub's treatment was called constraint-induced therapy (CIT) and a larger later experiment found it superior to normal stroke therapy. Consequently, Taub has been hailed by the American Stroke Association as "at the forefront of a revolution." But, due to the intensity of the regimen and the intensive hours required of therapists, CIT has not been widely adopted, especially in the United States, where insurance is not likely to cover the extensive therapy.

Though the insurance companies are slow, the evidence is clear. Our brain can reorganize itself. Just ask Lorie.

So if you or a loved one experiences some type of brain trauma, be sure to press medical personnel for all the options and therapies. Perseverance pays.

22. NEUROGENESIS

Despite even recent thoughts to the contrary, we can generate new brain cells, but not in the way we expected.

So what about these new brain cells? Do we really have all we are going to get by the time we're an adult? And if they aren't static, how does memory stay in place? How do we remember how to ride a bicycle if new cells are "tagged in" like wrestlers in a wrestling match?

Scientists knew neurons didn't divide, so they concluded new brain cell development was impossible.

And there were other reasons.

Considering the complexity of the brain, they couldn't imagine how new brain cells would assimilate. Expecting them to contribute "made as much sense as expecting a box of wires to improve an already running supercomputer."[54]

But what about Lorie? Did Lorie make new brain cells? And do older adults?

Animal studies were the first indications. In 1997 Fred Gage, Adler Professor in the Laboratory of Genetics at the Salk institute, conducted an experiment with lab mice using an enriched environment with steps, tunnels, wheels, toys, and lots of other mice. Other mice were placed in standard cages.

Compared to the standard cages, the enriched environment triggered the development of new neurons to the tune of 15 percent (from 270,000 neurons in the hippocampus to 317,000). It didn't matter how old the mice were. Senior citizen mice experienced even bigger boosts than the younger ones. The enriched environment, or something in it, was triggering the development of new brain cells, a process called "neurogenesis."[55]

At that time, neurogenesis was based only on animal studies, and wouldn't necessarily mean it would happen in humans. Human experimentation had significant roadblocks. For one, no form of non-invasive brain imaging existed to detect new neurons. And, animal studies involved euthanization to remove part of the brain for study under a microscope. Not an option for people.

Or was it?

Swedish neurologist Peter Eriksson, spending a sabbatical at Gage's lab, realized an opportunity may be available. Cancer patients were often injected with BrdU, a substance used to detect the spread of malignant cells. But BrdU would detect not only new cancer cells but also *any* new cell.

The light bulb went on. If BrdU could detect not only new cancer cells but any new cell, could it detect new neurons?

Eriksson sought permission from terminally ill patients and their families and physicians to do brain autopsies after patients had passed. Under the microscope he found BRdU tagged cells in the same location as neurogenesis was mapped in the animal studies. Patients had not received injections of BrdU until they contracted the disease, so cells marked by BrdU had to be generated after the injections.

Here was proof, contrary to prior dogma, that the adult human brain does generate new brain cells.[56]

Scientists were correct that brain cells do not divide, but new brain cells do come from another source. Our brains have a reserve called "neural stem cells," precursor cells capable of growing and differentiating into neurons and other types of nerve cells.[57]

So what causes neural stem cells to grow and differentiate into neurons and other cells? Back to the animal studies.

In a variation of the enriched environment experiment, Gage housed one group of mice in standard empty cages. Another group lived in cages with a running wheel they could use whenever they wished. (If you've ever had pet mice, you know the wheel would turn constantly all night!) The running mice produced twice as many new brain cells as the sedentary mice, suggesting physical activity alone generates new brain cells. After tweaking various environments Gage summarized his findings:

> We think voluntary exercise increases the number of neural stem cells that divide and give rise to new neurons in the hippocampus. But we think it is environmental enrichment that supports these cells. Usually 50% of the new cells reaching the dentate gyrus of the hippocampus die. But if the animal lives in an enriched environment, many fewer of the new cells die. Environmental enrichment doesn't seem to affect cell proliferation and the generation of new neurons, but it can affect the rate and the number of cells that survive and integrate into the circuitry. [58]

Gage continued such experiments and concluded running mice were also smarter.

But there was another variable of interest: the "voluntary" aspect. Gage conducted another experiment allowing one group of mice to get on and off the exercise wheel whenever they wanted. Another group was forced to stay on a mechanized treadmill or get thrown off like a rag doll. The conscripted mice did not display increased neurogenesis.[59]

So what does this mean for those couch potato friends of yours?

Well, dragging them involuntarily to the gym may be fruitless for brain capacity, but the exercise could still help in other ways. So maybe don't tell them about this experiment?

Following Gage's work, Brian Christie, of the University of British Columbia, zeroed in on the physical underpinnings of neurogenesis in the wheel-running mice. He found they also had more dendrites (the bushy little projections that receive signals from other neurons) and more spines on the end of the dendrites, thereby increasing sites by which they can receive signals from other neurons. In generalizing to humans, Christie surmised, "Exercise induced changes in brain structure [are] . . .

viable [ways] to combat deleterious effects of aging." This may well be why an active life benefits brain function.[60]

In fact, Lorie went through extensive physical exercise and mental stimulation throughout her rehabilitation. As an extra reward, she became an athlete.

So exercise is key. We don't have to become an athlete but we do need to keep moving to keep those new brain cells.

More on this and related concepts in later chapters.

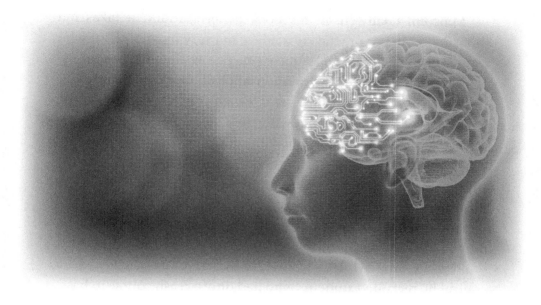

23. THOUGHTS COUNT

Thoughts can physically change the brain in beneficial ways.

So far we've seen the brain is much more malleable than before thought, and changeable through life experiences, at least of the physical kind.

But what about thoughts?

Remember Pascual-Leone's piano experiment, in which the brain recruited more cells based on just mental practice. Could the brain reorganize based on just thoughts? How do we tell? And how do we measure thoughts?

We know master musicians have increased brain real estate devoted to their skill. But what about masters of pure mental prowess? Or thought control? Comparing the masters with novices would help detect differences in brain patterns associated with thought control.

Malcolm Gladwell, in his book *Outliers*, found it takes ten thousand hours of practice to achieve mastery in a field. But who would have ten thousand hours of practice at thought control?

Monks. Monks who spend thousands of hours meditating.

Richard Davidson, PhD and noted neuroscientist at the University of Wisconsin, met with the Dalai Lama to discuss the science of the mind, and implications from the Buddhist perspective. The Dalai Lama was intrigued. He concluded that Buddhist concepts of mental transformation could be parallel with the plasticity of the brain.[61]

With the help of the Dalai Lama, Davidson recruited Buddhist monks to travel to Madison, WI, and meditate under his fMRI brain scan tube while he measured their brain activity. As a control he recruited students who had only a crash course in basic meditation techniques.

The monks showed significantly greater activity in the brain network associated with empathy than the novices.

But the most striking difference was the activity in the left prefrontal cortex, the site that marks happiness (more on this later). In the monks' brains, the left prefrontal cortex far exceeded activity of the right prefrontal cortex, the area associated with negative moods. By comparison, the control group showed no such difference. This was firm evidence that the "masters" could develop a change in neural patterns associated with happiness. Accordingly, Davidson suggests this positive state is a trainable skill.[62]

A trainable skill.

We can train ourselves to be happier. And we don't have to meditate for ten thousand hours. See chapters 35 through 37 for more on the science of happiness.

The following chapters will provide additional insight.

24. DIRECTED NEUROPLASTICITY

We can take action to direct our brain to change in desirable ways.

L et's think about Davidson's comment about happiness as a trainable skill. That's powerful. Are other mental states trainable as well?

Let's look at examples.

Jeffrey Schwartz at UCLA experimented with mindfulness based cognitive behavior therapy (MBCT) to see if it could quiet the circuits underlying obsessive compulsive disorder (OCD) behavior. He taught patients a type of mindfulness therapy based on Buddhist meditation, emphasizing paying attention to one's thoughts. He then conducted before and after brain scans to see if meditation had an effect. Activity in the part of the brain known for the OCD circuit dropped dramatically, and, in exactly the same manner as patients using prescribed drugs. Schwartz called it "self-directed neuroplasticity."[63]

Scientists at the University of Toronto conducted similar experiments by teaching depressed patients to view their thoughts differently. Fourteen patients underwent MBCT while thirteen others received Paxil, a standard antidepressant drug. They expected effects to be similar, and they were. All participants improved comparably after the experiment.

But the big surprise was the brain scans.

MBCT muted activity in the frontal cortex, the area where unwanted ruminations are seated. Paxil *raised* activity in the same place. MBCT increased activity in the "hippocampus of the limbic system" or the center of the brain's emotions. Paxil lowered activity here.

Toronto's Helen Mayberg explains, "Cognitive therapy targets the cortex, the thinking brain, reshaping how you process information and changing your thinking pattern. It decreases rumination and trains the brain to adopt different thinking circuits."[64] Later studies confirmed the improvements experienced by the MBCT patients were still present after two years. The patients on drugs needed to stay on them to maintain positive changes.

(Note these two studies were rooted in mindfulness-based *meditation*. Meditation is being taught in medical schools and in over two hundred fifty hospitals. It has been adopted by high-profile, successful people including Phil Jackson, Arnold Schwarzenegger, Rick Rubin, Tony Robbins, Ellen DeGeneres, Michael Jordan, Arianna Huffington, Rep Tim Ryan D-Ohio and many more. In fact, according to the National Center for Complementary and Integrated Health, about eighteen million adult U.S. citizens were practicing meditation in 2012. Many more are doing so now. If you are interested in more information on meditation, check out Appendix I.)

Educators are also experimenting. Seventh graders taught principles of neuroplasticity performed better on achievement tests than their peers.[65] Just knowing that your brain can change can be empowering.[66] Students found the revelations liberating and believed they could get smarter through study and practice.

Norman Doidge, author of *The Brain That Changes Itself,* says, "Everything to do with human training and education has to be re-examined in light of neuroplasticity."[67]

Richard Davidson pioneered another more direct experiment. He developed a "Kindness Curriculum" (KC) for preschoolers and kindergarteners that included age-appropriate mindfulness and loving-kindness meditation.

Children were given stickers and two envelopes: one for themselves and one with a picture of a sick child. They were told they could keep as many stickers as they wanted or they could also give some to the sick child. Over the course of the year, children in the KC group maintained initial levels of giving, while the control group became more selfish.[68]

In addition, compared to controls, the KC group developed significant gains in self-control, as measured by delayed gratification. Based on reports from teachers, they also ranked higher in learning, health, and social/emotional capacity compared to their peers. But more significantly, they also displayed more pro-social behavior and altruism. In summary, much can be done to direct our brain to rewire itself. Davidson's book, *The Emotional Life of Your Brain,* is an excellent source for methods to induce directed neuroplasticity. He explains development of emotional styles as well as the acquired skill of happiness. It's a highly recommended read. Davidson details specific meditation training to build attention, mindfulness-based training to deal with stress, and many other routines to build desired traits.

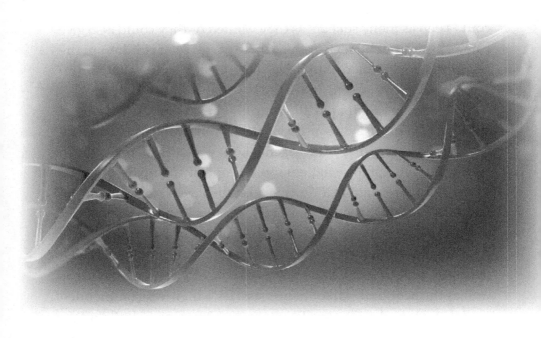

25. Epigenetics

Thoughts can change the way we express our genes.

We just found that thoughts can physically change our minds in substantial ways. But what about our initial foundation, our genetics? To what extent do our genes limit what we think and do?

Most of us would answer "a lot." We typically believe we were born with a set of genes that controls our lives, and we sense we are either victims or beneficiaries of those genes.

Evolutionary science supports these beliefs, implying much of human behavior is rooted in our evolutionary past. The science believes everything has an evolved purpose and explanation, which routes us right back to genetics, the code for how everything should unfold.

To be sure, our genes are significant. But how significant?

Brian Dias and Kerry Russel conducted a famous experiment at Emory University. They made mice afraid of one, and only one, fruity odor by pairing the odor with a mild shock. The fear-conditioned mice understandably developed more nose neurons sensitive to the smell. Then ten days after the fear conditioning, Dias and Russel allowed the mice to mate.

Here's the surprise: *Their offspring showed an increased startle to the fruity smell even though they had never been exposed to it.* And, they weren't fearful toward other smells.

Researchers then allowed the second generation of mice to mate and the same behavior surfaced in the third generation. The experiment was then repeated using *in vitro* fertilization, in case the parent mice were somehow training the offspring, even though the offspring had no contact with the fruity smell. The in vitro group yielded the same result. It proved the expression of genes was modified.[69]

In these experiments, researchers examined the *offspring* of mice to prove that *genes* were being modified. But gene expression is ongoing *in our own bodies* as our cells repair and reproduce. So modified gene expression is not limited to offspring. It could happen in our own bodies.

The same scientists found at least one mechanism responsible for this change in expression: DNA methylization. A methyl group (CH_3) is part of a larger organic molecule. Methylization occurs when methyl groups attach to millions of spots along the mouse genome and affects the expression of nearby genes.

The good news is we really don't need to understand the mechanics of methylization. We can treat it like a black box. We just need to know what goes in and what goes out. So the next question is what goes in to that black box or, in essence, what affects methylization?

The answer is straightforward. It boils down to the very human activities of aging, exercise, diet, smoking, environment, training, thoughts, and others. You can guess the good ones over the bad.[70]

This idea of gene expression being regulated by environment, training, thoughts, and other influences has triggered a new science called "epigenetics." And it's getting a lot of attention.

Bruce Lipton, PhD and former researcher at the Stanford University School of Medicine, takes issue with the hype surrounding the Human Genome Project. He thinks perceptions, thoughts, and beliefs have a bigger impact on people's health than their genes.[71]

Let's say that again. Perception, thoughts, and beliefs have a bigger impact on health than genes?

Lipton says genes continually adapt depending on the needs of cells in a changing environment. Even our perceptions can change the expression of our genes.

Lipton is not alone. Dr. Richard Davidson at the University of Wisconsin, one of the foremost researchers on the brain and emotions, describes genes as, "dynamic in their expression."[72] They can be turned up or down by our experience, environment, and training.

With the birth of epigenetics comes empowerment in shaping our brains. We don't have to be victims of our DNA.

Davidson says, "We have an extraordinary ability to transform our minds, if we so choose."[73] He continues, "We have far more control over our well-being, over how we respond to the world, than a simplistic deterministic view would permit."[74] The new science leaves us with a more optimistic message and even confers responsibility. It empowers us to take ownership of our own minds.

Taking more responsibility for our minds is not an entirely new idea. For years, Buddhists have viewed mental attributes— temperament, for example—as skills to be cultivated. The new science supports this perspective, telling us traits like resilience, attention, and social intuition are trainable. Davidson explores these issues in depth in *The Emotional Life of Your Brain* and the more recently published *Altered Traits,* by Goleman and Davidson. Refer to these books for more insight.

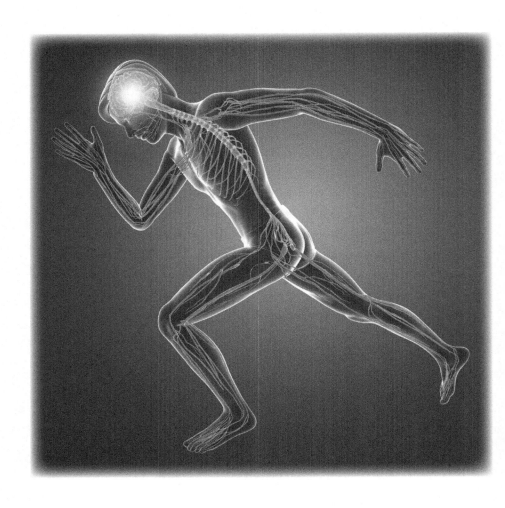

26. YOUR BRAIN ON EXERCISE

Physical exercise is essential for the health of our brain for a number of reasons.

The brain typically makes up 2 percent of our body weight. Take a guess how much energy your brain uses in proportion to your body.

Despite weighing a measly 2 percent of our body, the brain consumes a full 20 percent of the energy. That's a starting case for cardio to keep up the blood flow.

But remember how the exercising mice developed significantly more neurons? The evidence supports the same principle for adult humans.

Art Kramer at the University of Illinois found simple aerobic exercise or walking forty-five minutes three times a week improved episodic memory and executive control functions by 20 percent.[75] Likewise, a study in the journal *Neurobiology of Learning and Memory* found participants learned vocabulary words 20 percent faster after an intense workout as opposed to a low-impact activity.[76]

Science also suggests exercise is the best way to prevent or delay the onset of Alzheimer's.[77] A study published in May 2017, covering adults aged 60 to 88, found walking for thirty minutes four days a week, "strengthened connectivity in a region of the brain where weakened connections have been linked with memory loss."[78]

Beyond prevention of Alzheimer's, another study suggests "moderate intensity" exercise may even slow the aging of cells. As part of our life process, cells divide often. Part of the process involves "telomeres," or protective caps on the ends of chromosomes. As we age these protective caps get shorter. Once these caps become too short, they no longer provide protection and cells can no longer reproduce. We then have fewer healthy cells.

To study how exercise affects telomeres, scientists took muscle biopsies and blood samples from participants before and after a forty-five-minute exercise period. After exercise, the number of molecules protecting telomeres increased, thereby slowing the rate of shortening, and slowing the aging process.[79] Kramer found that a year of regular exercise—forty-five-minutes per day, three times a week—also improves memory, planning, dealing with ambiguity, and multitasking giving a seventy-year-old the connectivity of a thirty-year-old.[80]

End of chapter. I need to exercise and so do you.

27. YOUR BRAIN IN THE OUTDOORS

Your brain thrives on being outdoors.

Most of us enjoy being outdoors. But why?

In a study done at the University of Michigan, volunteers were randomly assigned to walk fifty minutes, either through an arboretum or city streets. Researchers then assessed participants' memory and attention through various cognitive tests.

Those assigned to the nature walk performed a full 20 percent better than their counterparts who walked the city streets.

The experiment was carried out both in June, with nice weather, and January, during the harsh Michigan winter. In both cases, the arboretum group yielded the same superior results.[81] And the arboretum group tended to be in a better mood.

Another study published in 2008 found that college students, when asked to repeat sequences of numbers back to researchers, were much more accurate after a walk in nature.

For further evidence researchers found that people immersed in nature for four days boosted their performance on a creative problem-solving test by 50 percent.

Beyond our cognitive abilities, a walk in the woods is good for our well-being as a whole. Japanese researchers sent eighty-four subjects for just a fifteen-minute walk in seven different forests while the same number were sent to walk around city centers. The forest walkers enjoyed significant relaxation. Overall, they had a 16 percent decrease in the stress hormone cortisol, a 2 percent drop in blood pressure, and a 4 percent drop in heart rate.[82]

Besides relaxation, being in nature can reduce ADHD symptoms. Frances Kuo, an associate professor at the University of Illinois, as published in the journal *Applied Psychology: Health and Well-Being*, found children who played a few hours regularly in an outdoor green environment displayed improved concentration and impulse control when compared to children who spent time indoors or surrounded by asphalt and pavement.[83]

Some of these health benefits could be provided by a chemical literally "in the air." From 2004 to 2012, Japanese officials studied the healing effects of "forest bathing" (essentially just spending time in a preserve of trees). Specifically, they measured the activity of human immune system natural killer (NK) cells before and after exposure to the woods. Test subjects showed significant increases in NK cell activity a week after a forest visit. And the positive effects lasted for a month. The result was at least partially attributed to inhaling phytoncides, essential oils trees emit into the air to protect themselves from germs and insects.[84]

Even if you can't get to the woods, it helps to just see trees. Rachel Kaplan, of the University of Michigan, found office workers with a view of nature were more satisfied with their jobs, had better health, and reported greater life satisfaction.[85]

Roger S. Ulrich, PhD and director of the Center for Health Systems and Design at Texas A&M University, found abdominal surgery patients recovered faster when their hospital rooms overlooked trees as opposed to patients whose rooms overlooked brick walls. Patients who could see nature had fewer complications, needed less pain medication, and got out of the hospital faster.[86]

So, if you can't smell the forest, at least find a window with a good view.

But it's not just forests or trees. Another outdoor experience is by the sea.

People have flocked to the beaches for ages, and, as it turns out, for good scientific reasons. *The Wall Street Journal* reports that salty air is good for you. Air near the ocean helps people clear out their lungs and reduces the need for antibiotics. Asthma sufferers report fewer and easier to manage attacks, and salt is naturally antibacterial. Acne, scrapes, cuts, or even internal inflammation are likely to heal faster with exposure to ocean air and water.

So sea air is good for your body. But what about your brain?

Researchers have found that just watching the ocean or other large body of water makes the brain release "awe" chemicals creating a sense of wonderment. Participants also felt more connected to nature and to the people with them.[87]

In summary, there's a reason that cabin in the woods or house on the lake or ocean is so expensive. Everybody wants one. And their desires are supported by science. But for those of us without the wherewithal to own property in the woods or on the beach, society has found it beneficial to provide public beaches and parks. Our brains will be thankful if we use them frequently.

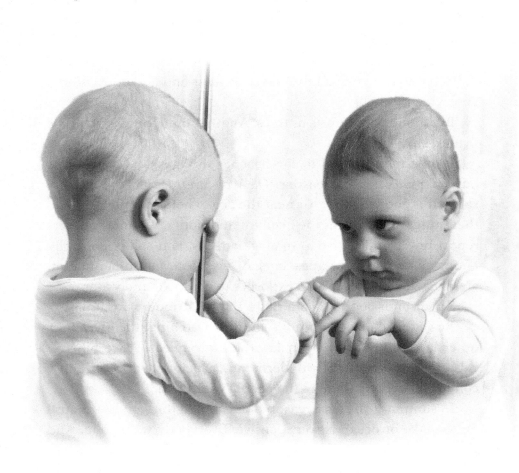

28. TALKING TO YOURSELF

Talking to yourself does help your brain in certain situations.

Do you ever talk to yourself when you are looking for something or trying to solve a problem? And then worry someone will hear you and think you are crazy?

You are not alone. And science has your back. There are *good* reasons.

A study published in the *Quarterly Journal of Experimental Psychology* by the University of Wisconsin divided participants into two groups. One was to search for food in the refrigerator or pantry while repeating out loud the name of the food. The other group was to search silently.

The result: People who talked to themselves found items faster than those who did not.

Study author, Gary Lupyan, explained, "The idea is that saying words out loud helped to activate properties more actively in the brain and efficiently configures your brain to help temporarily process the information. Language applies to all sorts of tasks that are not even consciously incorporated into these kinds of functions, like searching for objects."[88]

So if your significant other or roommate questions your sanity when you talk to yourself, tell them you're just activating more brain circuits to solve a problem. Then wait for "the look."

29. PAYING ATTENTION

Attention is a critical brain function and a skill that can be developed.

Pay attention. We hear the words all the time. We know it's essential to learning. But how does it work?

Back to the primates, but with a more humane experiment. Monkeys were wired to a device that made them tap their fingers one hundred minutes a day while listening to sounds on headphones. Some were rewarded with a sip of juice for responding to a change in the tapping rhythm. Others received the same reward for responding to a change in the sound. Every monkey had the same experience. The only difference was the impetus for the reward: attention to the sound versus attention to the physical tapping.

Results were compelling. Monkeys conditioned to pay attention to the physical tapping experienced an increase in the somatosensory (body movement) part of their cortex, but their auditory cortex stayed the same. The inverse was true for monkeys conditioned to pay attention to the sounds.[89] So attention is vital not only for learning but also for neuroplasticity.

From a learning perspective this is nothing new. We've all experienced the boring teacher or the topic incapable of capturing our attention. But remember learning is primarily considered the strengthening of connections or making new connections.

This experiment showed that expansion of physical cortex also depended on attention.

Attention is a big deal for our brain. It's both for learning and expanding cortical real estate. So how do we deal with attention or lack thereof?

"Only in recent years has Western psychiatry recognized attention-deficit disorder, but the meditative-contemplative traditions have maintained for thousands of years that we all suffer a kind of ADD and just don't recognize it," says Roger Walsh, a professor of psychiatry, philosophy, and anthropology at the University of California at Irvine.[90] Two thousand five hundred years ago the Buddha taught his followers to think of their mind as filled with dozens of monkeys all clamoring for attention. Meditation was meant to silence the monkeys. Can meditation in the vein of the Buddhist teachings help people diagnosed with ADD?

William Stixrud, PhD and clinical neuropsychologist, thinks it can.[91] Stixrud believes Ritalin, the typical drug used to treat ADHD, though helpful, is an imperfect treatment. Very few kids function optimally on it. Stixrud and Sarina Grosswald, an educator, studied Transcendental Meditation for ADHD children in a school setting. The kids meditated for ten minutes twice a day.

For these kids with ADHD an obvious question should be asked: "If kids have a problem focusing, how can they meditate?" Well, Transcendental Meditation, with roots in ancient Hindu practices, claims to be the exact opposite of focusing, using the natural tendency of the mind. See the appendix on meditation for more info. For now, let's just accept that they meditated.

Stixrud and Grosswald found the kids who meditated had 45 to 50 percent reductions in stress, anxiety, and depression. They also had significant improvements in organizational skills, memory, strategizing, mental flexibility, attention, and impulsivity.[92] Another two-year study showed children practicing Transcendental Meditation made significant gains on the Iowa Tests of Basic Skills, a nationally administered test to measure student progress in reading, science, math, language arts, and social studies.

Some schools are considering including meditation in daily routines, notably Roxbury Charter high and several other schools in Massachusetts.[93][94]

As noted earlier, "meditating increases the thickness of the cortex in the areas of the brain dealing with attention and sensory processing."[95] It can't hurt to have more brain real estate devoted to attention. In fact, meditation *could* be one drug-free tool for kids with ADHD and even boost the performance of other children. Studies have shown:

- Three thousand children in San Francisco Unified School District practiced Transcendental Mediation and made dramatic improvement in math test scores and overall academic performance.[96] The same study also found a decrease in student suspensions, expulsions, and dropout rates.

- A study at the University of North Carolina at Charlotte suggested meditation didn't have to be intensive to have an effect. Tests showed students could improve cognitive skills after just four days of meditation for twenty minutes per day. On one test, which measured sustained attention, meditating students did ten times better than a control group.[97]

- Another study found as little as two weeks of mindfulness practice produced a significant boost in GRE scores.[98]

Similar results are conceivable for adults who need their concentration at work.

Sixty adults participated in a study allowing them to attend a ninety-day meditation retreat, a long time for a retreat. Half could attend the ninety-day retreat right away, while the rest had to wait ninety days. The delay ensured results weren't related to just wanting to learn to meditate.

Testing was done before, during, and after the intensive retreat. All were asked to watch a series of lines flashed on a screen and click on a button when one line was shorter than the other—in other words, a really boring test. Detecting differences required intense focus. Those who meditated were more likely to see increasingly small differences in line length, and their abilities increased as their meditative training progressed. When they saw the differences, they didn't react faster than the control group, but they were more accurate. This would suggest that meditation helped with automatic processing of the visual signal, but not with reaction time.[99]

Another measure associated with attention is called "attentional blink."

A sample experiment will explain. Two pictures of dogs, a Scottish Terrier and a St. Bernard were embedded in a twenty-picture series of cats, each photo flashing in front of participants for a brief half second. Most people didn't see the second dog. Their attention "blinked." Scientists characterize this phenomenon as a misallocation of attention, thought to be a fixed property of the nervous system. Photos were flashing too fast for the brain to detect the second stimulus.

But another study showed that subjects who had meditated could improve the recognition rate for the second stimulus. Experienced and novice meditators were given attentional blink tests with two numbers embedded in a series of letters. The novice meditators tended to grasp the first number and hang onto it, thereby missing the second. The more experienced meditators didn't invest as much attention in the first number, as if letting go. This "release" resulted in better recognition of the second number. So, apparently, the ability to pay attention is not fixed, but a trainable skill.[100]

Video games present an interesting alternative as well. Richard Davidson's group developed a video game called *Tenacity* to train focused attention. They found, "increased connectivity between the brain's executive center in the prefrontal cortex and the circuitry for focused attention. In other tests, the players were also better able to focus on someone's facial expression and ignore distractions—signs of increased empathy."[101]

However, the verdict is still out on video games in genera.. Few have undergone stringent testing. Some have been found to improve performance in the game itself but not necessarily to generalize to other tasks. But the potential seems to be there for games written for specific attention tasks.

So how else can we invoke attention benefits?

Learn something new.

Activities we've practiced for a long time have minimal impact. But when we learn something new, we have to pay attention. Learning a foreign language or taking up ballroom dancing are much more likely to improve brain processing speed, strengthen synapses, and create functional networks.[102]

"Learning something new" could also apply to activities in which we are already engaged. But instead of doing the same old thing, we could get coaching, and learn to do it better. For instance, those of us who play bridge could take lessons to play differently and/or more effectively. Golfers, instead of hacking at the ball the same way (and yielding similar results), could hire a pro to learn a better swing. It would force us to pay attention, benefiting our circuitry.

In summary, the concept of attention is rich and complex. Science has found new possibilities beyond reward, high interest, and medication to help trigger attention benefits. Research will undoubtedly continue for this important dimension of our mind.

30. Increasing IQ?

IQ is not fixed as we once thought.
It is malleable like the rest of our brain.

In our lifetime, the most common measure of intellectual ability, IQ, has been thought to be stable. Scores were used to predict educational achievement and success in other facets of life. They were also used to assign children to advanced or remedial programs.

But is IQ really fixed? Since we've found the brain to be much more malleable, wouldn't it make sense for IQ to change, too?

Professor Cathy Price and her team at the University College, London, tested thirty-three adolescents in 2004 when they were between twelve and sixteen years old, and then retested four years later. On both occasions they also took structural brain scans using MRIs.

Contrary to the stable IQ theory, they found IQ could rise by up to 21 points or fall by as much as 18.

Think of the significance. A person jumping from 110 to 130 moved from "average" to "gifted."

The change wasn't just in performance. The study also showed IQ changes were linked to brain structural changes.

Thirty-nine percent of subjects whose verbal IQ changed significantly registered a corresponding change in the density and volume of gray matter activated by naming, reading, and speaking.

Twenty-one percent whose nonverbal IQ rose or fell registered corresponding density increases or decreases in the anterior cerebellum.[103] Interestingly, this site is also associated with moving the hand. In fact, other studies have found that refining your sensory-motor skills can improve cognitive skills.[104] This poses interesting questions about transferability and areas for new research.

Price and her colleagues could not establish the cause of IQ changes, since the measurements were done over time, without specific parameters, control groups, etc. But they could establish that intelligence *can* change. The questions remain: "How?" and "What activity transfers to another?"

Recent research found that short-term memory, the brain's scratch pad, may be key to raising overall IQ.

Susan Jaeggi of the University of Michigan conducted a study in 2008 that pointed to short-term memory as the foundation of pure intelligence. She and her colleagues trained adult volunteers on a difficult, complex short-term memory task. The more they practiced the short-term-memory task, the greater the improvement in what the researchers called "fluid intelligence," or the ability to reason and solve problems independent of existing knowledge. Building short-term-memory shows promise for increasing IQ and the commensurate skills.

Science does not have all the answers. But there are intriguing indications. Future research may significantly enhance our ability to learn to be smarter.

31. COGNITIVE RESERVE

---

*Cognitive reserve can be actively developed and is critical
for tolerating aging.*

In prior chapters, we established that exercising or doing new
or unfamiliar activities triggers changes in the brain, including
increases in connections between neurons, and even new gray
matter. Both contribute to what scientists call "cognitive reserve" or
"brain reserve." Research shows the more brain reserve, the more
resistant the brain is to age-related or disease-related damage like
Alzheimer's.

So we want all the cognitive reserve we can get. Then exactly what is cognitive reserve and how do we build it?

To better understand, envision flying in an airplane and looking down at two different scenes. One is a lush jungle, so dense you can't even see the ground. The other is only a few scraggly bushes growing on a desert. A healthy brain would be like the jungle with billions of connections between neurons. This condition is called "synaptic density" and is the primary measure of brain reserve.

When Alzheimer's or dementia invades the brain, the disease destroys synaptic connections. The more connections you have, the slower the progression of the disease—or at least the longer before you show symptoms.

Here's the interesting part: Research by autopsy has found significant numbers of people had the Alzheimer's pathology but never showed symptoms. The explanation was a build-up of significant brain reserves to either fight off or delay the onset of symptoms.[105] In other words, they had more "jungle" to impede the progress of the disease.

It turns out one of the best strategies for building up brain reserve is one of the toughest—no surprise, it *has* to be a challenge—learning a second language! A brain fluent in two languages must hold both languages active in the cortical circuits and then decide which one to use by way of the prefrontal cortex. The prefrontal cortex is the site of other higher order functions.

The workout it gets from bilingualism carries over, "buffing such IQ building skills as problem-solving and attention-switching," according to Ellen Bialystok of Canada's York University.[106] Bialystok reported such a workout appears to postpone dementia by five years!

Even more compelling is combining exercise of the body with a good brain workout. Remember exercise helps you develop more new brain cells. But most of these cells die off within two or three weeks. However, as the studies have shown, "animals that are trained to learn something new keep the cells alive."[107] So we generate new cells by exercising our bodies and keep more of those cells by exercising our brains.

Use it or lose it.

32. ACTIVITY AND ALZHEIMER'S

The more activity the better, strikingly so.

Dr. Yaakov Stern, leader of the Cognitive Neuroscience Division at the College of Physicians and Surgeons of Columbia University, has done significant research into building cognitive reserve. He found, regardless of age, occupation, or education, our level of participation in leisure activities has a significant and cumulative effect on establishing cognitive reserve. The more we do, and the earlier we start, the better the results.[108]

In 2001 Dr. Stern evaluated the effect of thirteen different activities combining intellectual, physical, and social elements. Most effective were reading, visiting friends or relatives, going to movies or restaurants, walking for pleasure, and going on an excursion. The group with a high level of activities had 38 percent less risk for developing Alzheimer's symptoms. And the kicker: The number of activities counts. For each additional activity, the risk was reduced by 8 percent.[109]

Consider activities with friends and relatives. Another study published in *Alzheimer's & Dementia: The Journal of the Alzheimer's Association* in 2008 explored the role of *social* activity by following 147 pairs of twins for an average of twenty-eight years. As with the Stern study, social engagement was an effective deterrent to Alzheimer's symptoms. Visiting relatives and friends, participating in a club, and attending parties were nearly as effective as cognitive tasks like reading.[110]

Author Dr. Michelle C. Carlson, an associate professor at the Johns Hopkins School of Public Health Center on Aging and Health, adds her perspective: "These activities might be indicative of an enriched environment, which has been shown in animal models to enhance the creation of new brain cells and promote brain repair."[111]

In 2008 Oscar Ybarra, PhD, a professor of psychology and management at the University of Michigan, found similar benefits for social engagement. He explains, "Social interaction involves many behaviors that require memory, attention and control. These mental processes are also involved in many cognitive tasks. Thus, social interaction would act as a prime, it would 'oil' these processes so that they are ready to be used when a cognitive task is to be solved."[112]

So maybe the teenage notion of studying with friends isn't totally without merit? Bad example. There's a time and place for everything. But activities and social engagement merit a time and place.

33. YOUR BRAIN ON LAUGHTER

*Though we instinctively know it, "no nonsense science" finds laughter
is exceedingly effective for our well-being.*

The last chapter covered activity and social engagement.
Being social and active also provides opportunities, one of
which has been called the "best medicine." When we are
with others, we are more likely to laugh.

Researchers at Loma Linda University showed a twenty-minute
laugh-inducing video to a group of healthy elderly people and an
elderly group with diabetes. A control group of similar elderly
individuals was not shown the video. The groups then completed
a memory assessment that measured learning, recall, and sight
recognition. They were also tested for levels of cortisol concentration before and after the experiment.

The results showed a significant decrease in cortisol concentration in both groups that watched the video. Likewise, the video-watchers showed greater improvement in all areas of memory assessment when compared to the controls.[113]

Cortisol damages certain neurons in the brain and can affect memory and learning. It also impairs the immune system. But laughter reduced cortisol levels thereby improving learning and memory, and, as a bonus, also improved the immune system. Scientists also found changes in brain wave activity towards the gamma frequency, which is known to amp up memory and recall.

We all love a good laugh and naturally seek sources. But maybe we should give ourselves even more chances. Could we take a break from the news, watch a comedy, or go out with our friends and laugh it up?

Still the best medicine.

34. Your Mind at Work

Relationships at work can be more important than job fit. And both relationships and performance can be enhanced with meditation.

The last couple of chapters covered activity, laughter, and interaction with our friends. But what about at work? What do those relationships mean for brain health? And, can brain training improve our performance at work?

A recent study in the journal *Personality and Social Psychology Review* set out to answer such questions. A meta-analysis covered fifty-eight studies and over nineteen thousand people with interesting results. Psychological and physical improvement wasn't necessarily about finding a job fitting one's personality and skills. Instead, researchers found "higher social identification with one's team or organization at work correlated with better health and lower stress."[114] Researchers surmised, "The positive psychological benefit may stem from the support provided by the work group but also the meaning and purpose that people derive from membership in social groups."[115] So when we look for that ideal job, we should interact as much as possible with people on our next potential team. That peer interview is for our benefit, too.

It isn't just relationships. We have to get work done, too.

Underlying our performance at work is a byproduct of nature, left over from our caveman days—the innate fight-or-flight response to stress. The brain diverts available energy away from the reasoning prefrontal cortex, to other parts of the body that enable a quick getaway from an attacking lion. Though we seldom worry about lions today, we invoke the same response with an overflowing to-do list or a sudden demand from our boss. To be productive, we need to calm the primordial stress reflex and engage the rational, thinking, executive part of our brain.

So how do we do that?

In a three-month-long study at a Fortune 100 company, employees who meditated improved significantly over matched controls on measures of overall effectiveness, job satisfaction, professional and personal relationships, and physiological "settledness." Meditators also noted decreased trait anxiety, job tension, insomnia, and cigarette and hard liquor use.[116]

A wholesale company compared those who practiced Transcendental Meditation for eight months to on-site controls. Those who practiced meditation scored higher on Leadership Practice Inventory tests than others. The Leadership Practice Inventory measures such things as vision, creativity, empowerment, and role modeling. Both meditators and non-meditators noticed changes in the meditators reflecting greater work effectiveness, increased energy, comfort taking initiative, and increased calmness in stressful situations.[117]

These benefits sound great, but you might ask, wouldn't a nap help just as much?

Researchers from the University of Kentucky, led by professor of biology Bruce O'Hara, provide insight.

Participants took a psychomotor vigilance test, a simple measure of reaction time. Subjects took tests before and after spending forty minutes in casual conversation, reading, sleeping, or meditating. Scores improved only after meditating. In fact, twelve of twelve subjects improved following meditation.[118]

Corporate America is catching on to Transcendental Meditation's effectiveness. Oprah Winfrey pays out of her own pocket for employees to learn Transcendental Meditation. Likewise, Ray Dalio, CEO of the world's largest hedge fund, spends forty minutes of his valuable time, every day, practicing meditation.[119]

Beyond performance at work, meditation may also help in the things most important outside of work. Just a few minutes of a meditation called "loving-kindness" increased positive connected feelings toward others per a study published in the journal *Emotion*.[120] Likewise, research at University of California at Berkeley suggests "mindfulness training makes couples more satisfied with their relationship, makes each partner more optimistic and relaxed, and makes them more accepting and close to one another."[121]

Meditation deserves attention in modern life and organizations could benefit by offering meditation training and allowing time to practice it. See the meditation appendix for more information.

When considering work and relationships, the conversation wouldn't make sense without factoring in attitude. Which of us has never griped about another employee with a "bad" attitude? The mix of culture, attitude, and work relationships is incredibly important, not only for our own health, but also for that of the organization. A recommended read for employee, manager, or owner is *Thank God It's Monday!: How to Create a Workplace You and Your Customers Love* by Roxanne Emmerich.

Emmerich shares a road map for developing a culture of shared values that vanquishes "bad" attitudes, and leads us to question not only our workplace norms but also our own. Let's face it. Our nature is to concentrate on changing other people's attitudes. And while it's possible to build an environment conducive to doing so, it's best to start with our own. Our own attitude has a lot to do with our well-being and performance.

The next chapter will help.

35. ATTITUDE & POSITIVE EMOTION

*Positive emotions have brain benefits well beyond the
"feel good" aspects.*

What about the self-help books touting positivity and changing attitude? Does your brain change as a result?

Let's first define positivity. Barbara Fredrickson, PhD, Kenan Distinguished Professor at the University of South Carolina at Chapel Hill, did extensive research and published many academic papers and a highly recommended book, aptly titled, *Positivity*. She defines positive emotions specifically as "joy, gratitude, serenity, interest, hope, pride, amusement, inspiration, awe, and love."[122]

OK. So how do they help?

Beyond the obvious feel-good aspects of positive emotions is a key concept: These emotions can *interact* with the reasoning, cognitive parts of our brain. Dr. Richard Davidson states, "When positive emotion energizes us, we are better able to concentrate, to figure out the social networks at a new job or new school, to broaden our thinking so we can creatively integrate diverse information, and to sustain our interest in a task so we can persevere."[123]

Along with broadening thinking, positivity broadens our attention. To support this claim, scientists at Brandeis University conducted a unique experiment with sophisticated eye-tracking equipment. Volunteers viewed pictures on a computer while their eye motions were photographed at a rate of sixty times per second. Half of the group randomly received positivity "injections," meaning they were influenced by an action known to cause positive emotions, like a funny story or receiving a piece of candy. The other half received nothing.

The positively influenced participants looked around more and spent more time on pictures on the periphery. Positive emotions literally affected the participants' physical propensity to take in more of their surroundings.[124]

Beyond attention, positivity "opens us up" producing a more open and curious mindset. Fredrickson notes, "The first core truth about positive emotions is that they open our hearts and our minds, making us more receptive and more creative."[125] Scientists have shown that a more open mindset produces a more accurate mental map of the world.[126] And, as you would expect, people with a more accurate mental map of the world navigate it more effectively.

A scholarly meta-analysis reviewed nearly three hundred different scientific studies covering over two hundred seventy-five thousand people and concluded that positivity produced success in life, whether it was measured by a satisfying marriage, a larger salary, or better health. The work supported the theory that positivity physically alters our brain and changes how we interact with the world.[127]

Positivity can also affect relations with others. Experiments show people are notoriously poor performers in recognizing faces across racial lines. Unfortunately, that ugly, racist phrase, "They all look alike to me," is supported by scientific experiments. But in recent studies, scientists discovered positive emotions help. In Fredrickson's words, "Positive emotions didn't simply diminish the entrenched racial bias, it eliminated it altogether: under the influence of positivity, people became just as good at recognizing individuals of another race as they were at recognizing individuals of their own race."[128]

The power of positive thinking also extends to the workplace. This seems instinctive but science backs it up. The Gallup Organization found that employees who regularly receive positive feedback: 1) increase individual productivity, 2) increase engagement among their colleagues, 3) have better safety records and fewer accidents on the job, 4) are more likely to stay with the organization longer, and 5) receive higher loyalty and satisfaction scores from customers.[129]

If improving our performance, broadening our thinking, improving concentration, creating more pathways to success, and improving our relations with others isn't enough, studies also show people who express more positivity live longer, by as much as ten years![130]

This longevity may be due to several factors. Remember earlier evidence concluding social activity and connectivity help prevent dementia and improve health? Well, positivity increases connectivity.

An experiment by Fredrickson and her students asked volunteers to describe their relationship with their best friends by overlapping circles. They then "injected" positivity and found volunteers saw more overlap between themselves, their best friends, and others. The experiment was replicated in other cultures as well. People feel more connected to the important people in their lives under positivity. It's more energizing to those around us and contagious as well.[131]

Positivity can also cause an increase in resilience, or the ability to quickly bounce back from life's challenges.[132] An experiment done by Christian Waugh, now at Stanford University, illustrates. Researchers measured participant levels of resilience using a psychological assessment. Then they showed the subjects either disturbing or neutral photographs while monitoring heart rate and blood pressure. Those with resilient personality styles reacted just as intensely to the disturbing photographs as those with non-resilient personality styles. However, the cardiovascular systems of the resilient participants recovered much more quickly than the non-resilient participants.[133]

Clearly, resilience is a desirable trait. So how do we build it?

Resilient people react to what is happening now without worrying about the future. They cut out advance worry and focus on the present moment and quickly "let go" of bad experiences.

This sounds a lot like mindfulness, a meditation technique. (See appendix on meditation.) And, in fact, studies have shown mindfulness training can improve resilience.

So, yes. All those self-help books about a positive attitude have a point. The question then becomes, "How do we attain these positive emotional states?" Meditation is one way. But others are available. We'll discuss more in the next chapter.

36. Creating Positivity

We can actively create positivity as opposed to waiting for it to come into our lives.

How do we inject positivity into our lives, specifically the positive emotions? Methods are surprisingly simple but not obvious.

We think if we see something funny or amusing, we will experience a positive emotion and smile. *But communication between the body and the brain runs in both directions.* So the act of smiling, in itself, can induce positive emotions. It seems backwards, but physically smiling triggers positive emotions by signaling back to the brain.

One study had participants hold a pencil horizontally with their teeth, forcing a smile. Other participants held the pencil in their lips, with one end hanging out, making it impossible to smile. Volunteers were then asked to rate cartoons. Those forced to smile found the cartoons significantly more humorous than those with the pencil hanging from the lips.[134]

Other examples of bidirectional communication are body posture and motion. Dr. Erik Peper of San Francisco State University had one group of subjects skip, swinging their arms upward as they made their way down a hall. Others slouched when they walked down the same hall. Almost all the skippers reported feeling more energetic, happy, and positive while the slouchers reported opposite emotions such as sadness, loneliness, isolation, and zombie-like feelings.

Peper discovered body posture also affects the recall of positive or negative memories. Participants sitting in a collapsed position, looking downward found it easier to recall hopeless, helpless, powerless, and negative memories. But when they sat upright and looked upward, it was nearly impossible to recall negative memories and much easier to recall empowering, positive memories.[135]

Positive language also works. Emmet Velten asked participants to read statements that were progressively more depressing or progressively more elating. As expected, after the readings, subjects then felt genuinely worse or better.[136] It seems obvious and we instinctively know this will happen, but we often forget we can use positive language to our advantage, such as reading an uplifting book for a boost in spirit or hanging around with a positive friend. This solution is obvious, but the next is not.

Reading or thinking faster is another way to promote a positive mood. Emily Pronin of Princeton and Daniel Wegner of Harvard combined Velten's mood induction procedure with their own speed-of-thought manipulation. They took 144 Princeton students and asked half to read progressively depressive phrases and half to read progressively elating phrases. But they also subdivided these groups with half reading slowly and half reading faster. As expected, the groups reading faster rated their positive emotions more favorably than slower reading groups. But, in an unexpected outcome, the fast readers in the depression group rated their emotions just as positively as the slow readers in the elation groups.

The study doesn't answer the question of why. But the authors theorize it may not be neurons firing faster, but the effort of quicker reading could distract the reader from negative thoughts. Put another way, when the brain is occupied with a difficult task, it doesn't have time to process other tasks, such as harboring negative feelings.[137]

Positive emotions can also be increased by hanging around with positive people. A study in *The British Medical Journal* concludes that happiness is contagious. Researchers tracked 4,700 people, originally as a twenty-year heart study. But by sifting through the data, they found happiness was transferred among groups of people, even to total strangers. The transferred happiness was good for up to a year.[138]

So we can hang around with our cheerful friends. Or find cheerful strangers! Then express gratitude for those cheerful friends or anything else right in our life.

Fredrickson notes that we can't just "put on" positive thoughts. We need certain "levers," as she calls them, to induce the positive emotions. One such lever is to ask ourselves questions, as in, "What things are going right in my life?" If we take time to come up with meaningful, positive answers, the positive feelings will follow.[139]

Then take the flip side. When we're haunted by a thought like, *What's going wrong with my life?*, we can challenge it, just like a trial lawyer.[140] We can ask questions like, "What started this thought?", or "How real is this possibility"? Or, "What are the facts?" "Are they just assumptions?" Also consider the negativity we receive from TV and other media and how it may impact our thinking. In Part One we discussed how our brain fools us and how we can't believe all we think. Is our brain fooling us now? What are the real facts?

Knowing we are thinking negative thoughts is part of the battle. This is where mindfulness shines. It's more than a type of meditation. It's learning to take a step back and calmly observe our thoughts. By doing so we learn to accept a thought as just a thought. It's just an occurrence that originates in our mind and then soon passes. Mindfulness is learning to observe thoughts, accept them, and then let them dissipate. By doing so we can learn to accept our thoughts, even the negative ones, without having a bodily emotional reaction. See the appendix on meditation for more on mindfulness and course information.

Speaking of meditation, simply repeating a mantra can change our state of mind and make us happier and less stressed. A 2015 study in the journal *Brain and Behavior* showed how the brain changes in the areas related to happiness when we repeat a mantra.[141] Positive phrases like, "I am at peace in the world," or "I can get through this," build stronger connections in the areas of our brain associated with happiness.

Gratitude, as noted above, is another big positive influence. Robert Emmons of the University of California at Davis randomly assigned one thousand adults to one of three groups. The first kept daily journals of their moods and rated them on a scale of 1 to 6. The second group did the same but also listed annoying or distracting things. The third also kept the mood journal but wrote down things for which they were grateful.

Despite random assignment, the third group had the predictable jump in overall feelings of happiness. But they also spent more time exercising, having regular checkups, and taking other preventative health measures. The self-induced grateful people were more likely to see life and health as a gift and take care of themselves[142] Not surprisingly, the difference was most pronounced compared to the group focused on life's hassles.

Sonja Lyubomirsky, at University of California at Riverside, under a grant from the National Institutes for Health, also found gratitude journals significantly increased satisfaction with life. The improvements were maintained over six weeks when compared to a control group with no journals.

Emmons, at University of California at Davis, found gratitude exercises improved physical health, too. It raised energy levels, and, for patients with neuromuscular disease, relieved pain and fatigue.[143]

Positive emotions can be injected into our lives in a variety of ways, and the benefits are proven. We need to be aware of opportunities and take time to use and enjoy them.

37. A Science of Happiness

Psychologists have now created a science of happiness and it can be associated with a definite physical state of the brain.

In previous chapters we've discussed positive emotions, which lead to at least some form of happiness. But is that all there is to it?

Long ago, prior to the year 180 AD, Roman Emperor Marcus Aurelius provided relevant insight, but in ways he could not see in his time. One quote is especially prescient: "failing to understand the workings of one's own mind is bound to lead to unhappiness." This implies that understanding how your mind works *can* lead to happiness. The second quote drives this home, "it is all within yourself in your way of thinking."

Yet, despite Marcus Aurelius' insight 1,900 years ago and the 1776 U.S. declaration of "an unalienable right," only in the last twenty years has science even started efforts to understand "happiness."

In 1992, the Dalai Lama, hearing about Richard Davidson's cutting edge research on the brain and emotions, posed, "Scientists often study depression, anxiety and fear, but why not devote your work to the causes of positive human qualities like happiness and compassion?"[144] Since then Davidson has taken up the challenge.

Likewise, Martin Seligman, in 1998, as a newly elected president of the American Psychological Association (APA), declared psychologists needed to study what makes people happy. Seligman said, "I realized that my profession was half-baked. It wasn't enough for us to nullify disabling conditions and get to zero. We needed to ask, 'What are the enabling conditions that make human beings flourish? How do we get from zero to plus five?'"[145] Thus began the science of what makes us happy.

Early on, the spending of precious scientific research dollars on esoteric concepts like happiness was considered a wasteful venture, making it difficult to attract funds. But as research began to report improved immune systems, longer life expectancy, and increased productivity, the funding became much more available. The promise of reduced medical expense and increasing productivity found open minds and more research dollars.

So what is happiness?

Davidson calls happiness "a kind of a placeholder for a constellation of positive emotional states . . . associated with an active embracing of the world. . . . "[146] But it is not just an indefinite, ambiguous feeling. Davidson says it's a physical state of the brain, one that can be induced deliberately.[147] Scientifically speaking, that physical state is characterized by increased activity and circuitry in the left prefrontal cortex, as identified by magnetic resonance imaging (MRI) and electroencephalograms.[148]

In fact, some people are genetically predisposed to happiness by virtue of busy prefrontal cortexes. Research on infants has provided confirmation. Davidson measured left prefrontal cortex activity in babies less than a year old with their mothers present, and then again when their mothers briefly left the room. Some babies cried hysterically the minute the mother left. Others were more resilient. The babies with the higher activity in the left prefrontal cortex were the ones who didn't cry.[149] As many parents can attest, some babies are just born to be happy.

But neuroscientists also know, as we learned in the chapter on neuroplasticity, the brain is highly plastic. The brain rewires itself in response to experiences, and Davidson's research has shown just how plastic it can be. His study of Buddhist monks in a meditative state found activity in the prefrontal cortex shot up at a dramatic rate, a rate he had never seen before. Science continues to delve into the physical underpinnings of the state of happiness, confirming that happiness is a trait or state that can be physically measured and learned.

A happy brain can also have a powerful physical influence over the rest of the body. People who score on the upper ends of psychological tests for happiness develop about 50 percent more antibodies than average in response to flu vaccines.[150] Other researchers have found related mental states such as hopefulness, optimism, and contentment "appear to reduce the risk or limit severity of cardiovascular disease, pulmonary disease, diabetes, hypertension, colds, and upper respiratory infections as well."[151]

Clearly, as the Dalai Lama suggested, the state or trait of happiness is well worth studying and learning.

But is happiness only induced by positive emotions?

Seligman says there is more. According to his work, we can experience three kinds of happiness:

1) pleasure of positive emotion,
2) engagement, absorption, and goal directed behavior, and,
3) meaning and purpose, belonging to something larger than oneself.[152] [153]

We've covered the first in the last couple of chapters. We won't repeat.

The second type of happiness, "The Good Life," is about experiencing the pleasure of achieving a goal or the sense of accomplishment in finishing a task. In our culture we are expected to improve skills or develop talents, and many resources are available to aid in this work. We are taught from early childhood to explore our strengths and spend more than the first quarter of our lives learning to be productive. We won't explore this type of happiness further as countless books are available on developing our talents and becoming more effective. One timeless resource is *The Seven Habits of Highly Effective People* by Stephen Covey. Another, more applicable in a work group setting, is *Thank God It's Monday* by Roxanne Emmerich. Whether it's "sharpening your saw" or "having the talk" (references from the books), we can find helpful information to become more effective and accomplish our goals.

The third type of happiness, "The Meaningful Life," is about meaning and purpose and belonging to something larger than oneself. It's been associated with altruism, or kindness and giving. Dr. Christopher Peterson at the University of Michigan, one of the founding fathers of positive psychology, says, "When you're volunteering, you're distracting yourself from your own existence, and that's beneficial. Giving puts meaning into your life. You have a sense of purpose because you matter to someone else."[154]

Science has detected the physical evidence of this impact. Dr. Jordan Grafman of the National Institute of Neurological Disorders reports, "Scans show that the brain structures that are activated when you get a reward are the same ones that are activated when you give. In fact, they're (the giving ones) activated more."[155] So giving triggers responses in our brain that make us happy. We've all experienced that feeling. It's called "helper's high." Writing a letter to a grandparent, visiting a nursing home, helping a friend's child with homework, or mowing a neighbor's lawn are all good things that can bring that satisfaction. But while it's simple enough to give, can we do things to enhance *our capacity* for such kindness and giving?

Dr. Richard Davidson solicited volunteers with no previous meditation experience and randomly assigned them to learn either compassion meditation or a structurally matched derivation of cognitive therapy. Guided practice for both groups was provided online for thirty minutes a day for two weeks. At the end, participants were asked to make economic decisions to measure altruism. These decisions involved real money where the participants lost money if they chose to be more altruistic. Compared to the cognitive therapy group, the compassion group was more pro-social and chose to give up more money, suggesting that as little as seven hours of compassion meditation triggers measurable differences.[156]

A *New York Times* article from December 2017 found similar results with school children. P.S. 212 in Queens installed the Kindness Curriculum developed by the Center for Healthy Minds at the University of Wisconsin. Preschoolers were introduced to mindfulness through sensory games, stories, and songs designed to help them pay attention to their emotions. This program has attracted a lot of attention. Since its release in August 2017 over fifteen thousand educators, parents and others from around the world have signed up.

Psychologist Lisa Flook administered tests showing that youngsters receiving the kindness training were more altruistic in their willingness to share with others and also more focused while achieving modest gains in academic performance.[57] The more aware the children were of their own emotions, the better they could empathize with the feelings of others and respond helpfully.

This Kindness Curriculum is part of a growing global movement to teach emotional intelligence in schools, skills that can be as important as math and reading in engaging the world and flourishing. But it's not just learning to flourish. Kindness to others adds meaning to our lives. And the search for meaning is a powerful contributor to happiness. The following quote summarizes eloquently:

> A human being is a part of a whole, called by us the Universe, a part limited in time and space. He experiences himself, his thoughts and feelings, as something separated from the rest, a kind of optical delusion of his consciousness. This delusion is a prison for us, restricting us to our personal desires and to the affection for a few persons nearest us. Our task must be to free ourselves from this prison by widening our circles of compassion to embrace all living creatures and the whole of nature in its beauty. —Albert Einstein[58]

In summary, the new science of happiness supports those things we knew made us better people. Besides creating positive emotions as in the preceding chapter, it's about engagement and absorption and goal direction. It's also about finding meaning and purpose and belonging to something greater than oneself. So volunteering and belonging to service organizations or taking classes to learn something new or doing whatever it takes to reach your goals are steps in the right direction.

38. YOUR BRAIN ON MONEY

Sure money matters, but your brain may process it differently than you think.

We've covered altruism and a number of esoteric concepts regarding happiness. But let's get practical for a moment. What about money? How does it affect happiness?

We've all heard the old phrase, "Money doesn't make you happy." But we spend much of our time and talent learning to make money. So can it be that simple?

It can cut both ways. And maybe not in the ways we typically expect.

First, the tried and true about buying happiness. Dan Gilbert, a psychology professor at Harvard, says, "Once you get basic human needs met, a lot more money doesn't make a lot more happiness."[159] Research shows going from earning less than $20,000 per year to more than $50,000 makes you twice as likely to be happy. But exceeding $90,000 makes very little incremental difference.[160] Part of the reason is we overestimate the satisfaction we get from "things." Though we initially get a thrill from the new car or the large screen TV, we soon get used to it and just go back to the mall for more.

However, money spent in certain ways can make us happier. A *Money* magazine video notes people of all income levels became happier when they spend money on things to save time. Likewise, spending money on engaging activities (like vacations) makes us happier than buying things. Researchers theorize our experiences tend to "blossom" in our memories as we recall them, not diminish. We edit out the bad cab ride and remember the glorious sunsets.[161] So don't skip the vacation just because planning is a hassle.

Another money-related problem is our propensity to compare ourselves to others. Happiness scholars found the size of our paycheck relative to others makes a much bigger difference than simply the amount of our earnings.

Dartmouth College economist Erzo Luttmer matched census data with a national survey of self-reported happiness and found our neighbor's paycheck significantly impacted our own happiness! Luttmer says, "If you compare two people with the same income, with one living in a richer area than the other, the person in the richer area reports being less happy."[162]

So the bottom line on money and happiness is "enough" helps. If we have more than enough, we could spend it on saving time and *doing* things, not *accumulating* things. We could hang with friends who don't "spend it up," and live in a neighborhood well within our means. And, if we have more than enough, we could consider what we could do to help others, Seligman's third type of happiness.

39. YOUR BRAIN ON RELIGION: NEUROTHEOLOGY

Despite the typical arguments about religion, it could be helpful to your mind and health.

The May 7, 2001 cover article of *Newsweek* featured a study discovering the part of the brain responsible for religious experiences. This could imply that God is just in our heads. However, there is a valid argument.

The authors, Sharon Begley and Anne Underwood, state in their final paragraph, "But it is likely that they will never resolve the greatest question of all—namely, whether our brain wiring creates God, or whether God created our brain wiring. Which you believe is a matter of faith."

Do you sometimes envy people with strong faith? Do you wish it were that simple for you? Do you have trouble reconciling religion with science? Or with everyday experience?

Those are reasonable questions. Even the Dalai Lama wrestles with such issues. Matthieu Ricard, who has a PhD in molecular biology and is a Buddhist monk, offers, "the Buddha always said that one should not accept his teachings simply out of respect for him, but rediscover their truth through our own experience, as when checking the quality of a piece of gold by rubbing it on a piece of stone, melting it and so on."

Likewise, other religious leaders have promoted the value of questioning. Jim Wallis, spiritual advisor to former President Obama, said it well, "Real faith, you see, leads us to deeper reflection and not—not ever—to the thing we as humans so very much want . . . *easy certainty*."

This chapter briefly explores dimensions and beliefs and applies our recent science awareness to admittedly scientifically unanswerable questions. It's not about conversion to a religion. It's about applying science and logic and questioning our beliefs.

Don't get the wrong impression. It's not about turning loose of your faith. Science tells us religion can be a very good thing.

For one, it could make us happier. The truth is people with a spiritual commitment or a high level of faith and devotion are twice as likely to report being "very happy" than spiritually non-committed people. High religiousness also predicts lower risk of depression and more reports of well-being and satisfaction with life. Jeffery Kluger of *Time* magazine says, "a growing body of evidence suggests that faith may indeed bring us health. People who attend religious services do have a lower risk of dying in any one year than people who don't attend. People who believe in a loving God fare far better after illness diagnosis than people who believe in a punitive God."[163]

You'll remember from prior chapters the power of gratitude in promoting happiness. Religious people may be happier because they are better trained in gratitude. Religions often teach gratitude in prayer and other ways. Likewise, religion offers a sense of community and connectedness that we found so important in earlier chapters. And, religion promotes altruism, leading to a sense of meaning, the third source of happiness.

So religion is worth our attention. And scientists haven't missed the message.

Carl Sagan, perhaps one of our greatest scientists, provided interesting insight:

> How is it that hardly any major religion has looked at science and concluded, 'This is better than we thought! The Universe is much bigger than our prophets said, grander, more subtle, more elegant?' Instead they say, 'No, no, no! My god is a little god, and I want him to stay that way.' A religion old or new, that stressed the magnificence of the universe as revealed by modern science might be able to draw forth reserves of reverence and awe hardly tapped by conventional faiths.

In fact, science has become more complex since Sagan's writing. The discovery of the potential for multi-universes and the Higgs boson, or "God particle," has scientists in complete awe and respect for what we do not yet know.

With the discovery of "inflation," the phenomenon where the universe expanded exponentially in the first trillionth of a second on a scale incomprehensible to us mere humans, it's hard to not envision an awesome superior intelligence. Yet, fundamentalist Christians and others who take the Bible literally, or "creationists" don't see inflation as scientific support for their claim that God created the universe. Their God took seven days, not trillionths of a second.

Scientists believe there was evolutionary pressure for religion. And it's no secret that early church leaders enacted doctrines to keep their followers "in line."

Knowing this, the Dalai Lama has countered that the purpose of religion is to control yourself, not others. It may not be a bad thing to question dogma born of exclusion and lack of love, or to question churches telling us gays do not belong or that a divorced person cannot be married in the church. These are the "precepts of men," arising from religious desires to control or keep people in line.

However, despite the control issue, religions have enabled people to band together and help each other and "do good." Dr. Andrew Newberg, an associate professor of radiology and psychology at the University of Pennsylvania, states in an interview for *The SharpBrains Guide to Brain Fitness*,

> We shouldn't throw the baby out with the bathwater. I don't think religion is a black and white matter: yes, fundamentalism is a problem, as is rejecting data and ignoring scientific findings. But there are also good elements: the motivation to care about human beings, to develop compassion, to perfect ourselves and the world. [164]

People have given up on religion due to disagreements on doctrine or dogma. Those disagreements are likely healthy. But we shouldn't consider them reasons to disregard religion altogether.

There are reasons to persevere.

From a self-serving perspective, people with stronger religious beliefs do seem to have better health, resilience, and mental well-being. And, as shown in earlier chapters, the sense of community available from a church congregation can be beneficial. Likewise, the opportunities for altruism and living Seligman's "good life" or "meaningful life" are usually more available in religious organizations. Most have missions or community improvement projects or programs for less fortunate people to which members may contribute their time or money.

But there are those disagreements with church dogma. Let's look at it another way: a disagreement with a family member over politics or another point of view isn't a reason to leave the family. Perhaps, it's the same with religions. Their policies or precepts may not be "right," but if they are not doing harm, and they are doing good for you and others, maybe you should consider the relationship like your family.

See the appendix on religion for additional discussion and an attempt to find an "essence."

RECOMMENDED READING PART TWO

1. *The Emotional Life of Your Brain* by Richard Davidson, PhD, and Sharon Begley is written by one of the most respected researchers in the field along with one of the most respected science writers. The subtitle is descriptive: "How Its [the brain's] Unique Patterns Affect the Way You Think, Feel, and Live—and How You Can Change Them." This book provides significant detail beyond our discussion. It's highly recommended for the "next read" on this topic.

2. *Positivity* by Barbara L. Fredrickson, PhD, discusses positive emotions in more depth and offers additional "levers" to create them.

3. *Altered Traits* by Daniel Goleman and Richard J. Davidson combines two of the great minds in this area of research. Davidson has already been mentioned. Goleman is the author of *Emotional Intelligence*, now considered as important as IQ. Davidson and Goleman critically review the research on meditation and provide scientific evidence to separate the proven from conjecture. Again, the subtitle is descriptive: "Science Reveals How Meditation Changes Your Mind, Brain, and Body."

Appendix I: Meditation

"Our life is what our thoughts make of it."

—Marcus Aurelius

Parade, the most read magazine in the United States with over 54.1 million readers, published an article titled, "The No.1 Health-Booster in 2015."[165] It reported mindfulness and meditation were the hottest trends in well-being, with celebrities, business moguls, and politicians touting its benefits. Major publications and news outlets such as *TIME* magazine, *U.S. News and World Report*, *Today*, *ABC News*, the *Chicago Sun Times*, and *The New York Times* ran special features. Even Rochelle, IL (a conservative rural town with a population of nine thousand) ran a cover article on meditation.

Health Benefits

Academia, medical facilities, and popular sites—such as Mayo Clinic, Carnegie Mellon University, University of Massachusetts Medical School, WebMD, and Psychology Today—have devoted major resources to getting the word out. They continue providing significant research, with over 2,200 papers published in the last five years on mindfulness.[166]

Many businesses have realized the productivity potential behind this healthy practice. Companies such as General Mills, Abbot Bioresearch, the Bose corporation, New Balance, and others have presented workshops for employees titled, "The Power of Mindfulness in the Workplace," a program developed by the University of Massachusetts Medical School Center for

Mindfulness. *Fortune* 500 companies including Google, AOL, Apple, and Aetna offer mindfulness and meditation classes on-site for employees.

Meditation is no longer viewed as a new age fad. It is a proven practice with significant health benefits.

In case you are still thinking, "but this is just for those artsy types," consider the successful people who use meditation.

- Let's start with Joe Madden, former manager of the World Series Champion Chicago Cubs, who was quoted as saying "I love to meditate in the morning. I'm a big believer in meditation."[167]
- Ray Dalio, billionaire founder of Bridgewater Associates, the largest hedge fund in the world, said, "Meditation, more than anything in my life, was the biggest ingredient of whatever success I've had."[168]
- The list of executives who meditate includes Ford Motor Company Chairman Bill Ford, News Corp CEO Rupert Murdoch, and Oprah Winfrey.[169]
- *Huffington Post* editor-in-chief Arianna Huffington, who meditates daily, calls it, "the third metric in success, after money and power."[170]
- Even government officials are embracing it. U. S. Rep. Tim Ryan (D-Ohio) holds weekly meditation sessions on Capitol Hill. [171]

Throw in a slew of marquee athletes of the present and past such as Michael Jordan, Steph Curry, and Phil Jackson, and you have a formidable case.

So why are these people and corporations embracing this ancient practice?

To quote Tim Ryan, whose goal is to infuse mindfulness into many of the institutions of our country, "Stress is bipartisan. Mindfulness cuts through current political divides: it's based on self-care and preventing illness. And increasing overall well-being can save healthcare dollars and promote individual responsibility."[172]

Let's dive deeper into the uses..

To ready your brain let's try a game. Study the following list and choose which you believe are benefits of meditation that are supported by scientific evidence.

1. Improving focus and reducing impulsivity in people with ADHD
2. Slowing, limiting the effects of aging
3. Treating alcoholism
4. Reducing anxiety and blood pressure
5. Assisting in cancer treatment
6. Lowering cholesterol
7. Increasing compassion
8. Treating depression
9. Decreasing fibromyalgia symptoms
10. Modifying gene expression or the way our body turns genes on or off
11. Relieving aches and pains
12. Hastening healing
13. Reducing the risk of heart disease and stroke
14. Improving IBS symptoms
15. Boosting the immune system
16. Increasing intelligence, gray matter
17. Improving psoriasis symptoms
18. Improving relationships
19. Boosting school performance
20. Promoting better sleep
21. Helping smoking cessation
22. Relieving stress
23. Increasing telomerase (a substance that helps telomeres protect chromosomes from damage)
24. Controlling weight
25. Increasing workplace efficiency

You've probably guessed, the correct answer is *all of them.* "No. I Health Booster," indeed.[173]

Family physicians estimate as many as two thirds of office visits are for stress-related symptoms, such as depression, anxiety, chest pain, panic disorder, etc.[174] In response to this "epidemic" of sorts, the University of Massachusetts sponsored the Mindfulness-Based Stress Reduction (MBSR) program, a type of meditation training. Participants undergo eight weeks of training and then maintain their own meditation practice afterward. The program has been running and studied extensively for over thirty years. Published outcomes show a 35 percent reduction in medical symptoms and a 40 percent reduction in psychological symptoms.[175]

Let's look at more specific outcomes.

MBSR training for cardiac rehabilitation reduced mortality by 41 percent for two years following the training.[176] Hypertension (high blood pressure) improved comparably to changes from medication, weight loss, sodium restriction, and aerobic exercise.[177] Likewise, studies found significant reductions in anxiety, depression, headache, and other stress-related symptoms.[178] A prominent article in *JAMA,* the official journal of the American Medical Association, concluded that mindfulness meditation could relieve anxiety, depression, and pain to the same degree as medications, but without the side effects.[179]

Jon Kabat-Zinn, a founder of the UMass stress reduction program, reported twenty of twenty-two anxiety patients recorded improvement and a 25 to 65 percent decrease in mean scores on Hamilton and Beck depression and anxiety scales. (Hamilton and Beck is a psychological questionnaire used by clinicians to assess the severity of depression and anxiety.) Gains were maintained at a three-month follow-up, and 90 percent still used the MBSR techniques at thirty months.[180] In addition, Davidson and Goleman, after reviewing many studies, found, "meditation can lead to decreases in depression (especially severe depression), anxiety and pain—about as much as medications but with no side effects."[181]

The MBSR program has been effective and is gaining popularity with programs available at major hospitals across the country.

Transcendental Meditation has also significantly impacted stress-related illness. As we discuss health related benefits, both Transcendental Meditation and MBSR will be included.

Scientists followed 201 African-American men and women diagnosed with coronary heart disease (CHD). Participants were randomly assigned to either a health education class about diet and exercise, or to attend a Transcendental Meditation (TM) program. After five years of follow-up, the meditation group had a 48 percent reduction in the overall risk of heart attack compared to the other group.[182]

Likewise, Dr. C. Noel Bairey Merz, from Cedars-Sinai Medical Center in Los Angeles, told *Reuters*, "CHD patients who want to 'do it all' for optimal risk reduction should consider learning and practicing TM™." The study provided Transcendental Meditation instruction to fifty-three adults with stable CHD while another fifty-one patients with similar symptoms received standard heath education. At the end of sixteen weeks patients in the Transcendental Meditation group had lower blood pressure and greater improvements in blood glucose and insulin levels. In addition, Transcendental Meditation practitioners had more stable heart rate variability, a sign of heart health.[183]

Transcendental Meditation studies have also shown significant effects on blood pressure. A meta-analysis of twelve studies with 996 participants showed "an approximate reduction of systolic and diastolic BP of -4.26mm Hg. . . . and-2.33 HG in TM™ groups compared with control groups. Results from subgroup analysis suggested TM™ had a greater effect on systolic blood pressure among older participants."[184] These studies have not gone unnoticed by professional organizations. The American Heart Association has now concluded that Transcendental Meditation lowers blood pressure and recommends it be included in clinical practice for prevention and treatment of hypertension.[185]

Another study in the *American Journal of Hypertension,* followed 298 college students who were randomly assigned to either a Transcendental Meditation group or a waiting list (control group). The study found Transcendental Meditation helped decrease psychological stress. But, more interestingly, a subgroup of students at risk for high blood pressure later in life showed lasting benefits in lower blood pressure.[186]

Building on these results, a study published in 1998 in *Psychosomatic Medicine* showed practitioners of Transcendental Meditation have lower levels of lipid peroxide than non-meditators. Lipid peroxide can contribute to atherosclerosis and other chronic diseases.[187]

Stress doesn't always lead to heart disease or hypertension, but the psychological effect can be just as debilitating. The occupational hazard known as burnout can be a problem in some professions. One is teaching. According to the National Commission on Teaching and America's Future, teacher turnover in the U.S. has risen to 16.8 percent and over 20 percent in urban schools. And 46 percent of new teachers leave the profession within five years. That has an impact not only on the teacher, but also on colleagues and students.

A study published in *Permanente Journal* gave cause for hope. Using the Maslach Burnout Inventory (a psychological inventory comprising twenty-two items pertaining to occupational burnout), researchers discovered a significant reduction in perceived stress, depressive symptoms, and teacher burnout after just four months of Transcendental Meditation.[188]

Sleep is also affected by meditation. A study from India's National Institute of Mental Health and Neurosciences focused on vipassana meditation, a type of meditation focusing on the relationship between mind and body. The essence is to observe thoughts and physical sensations but to avoid judgment. The study included 105 healthy men between age thirty and sixty. Half were experienced vipassana meditators and half did not practice meditation at all. The meditators experienced enhanced deep sleep and REM across all age groups. Non-meditators had a pronounced decline in slow wave sleep associated with age, typical for aging men.[189]

The early experiments on meditation covered healing, the immune system, and pain relief. Just over an hour of meditation training can have a dramatic impact on both the experience of pain, and physical brain activation related to pain, according to Dr. Fadel Zeidan, a neuroscientist at Wake Forest Baptist Medical Center.

Zeidan recruited a small group of healthy medical students to attend four twenty-minute training sessions on mindfulness meditation. To administer pain, they heated a small thermal stimulator to 120 degrees and applied it to the back of each volunteer's right calf. Subjects reported on unpleasantness and intensity of the pain. After meditation training, subjects reported a 40 percent decrease in pain intensity and a 50 percent reduction in unpleasantness. But it wasn't just their perception that changed.

The research team did MRI scans to measure activity in the somatosensory cortex. When participants first experienced pain without meditation training, the corresponding area in the cortex showed increased activation. After meditation training, activity in the same location was barely detectable. The brain images showed increased activation in the areas of the brain related to cognitive control and emotion, where the experience of pain is thought to be built. The better meditators had more activation in the areas of cognitive control and a lesser experience of pain.[190]

Another study on Zen meditation and pain conducted at the University of Montreal also explored why meditators are less sensitive to pain. By using MRI scanners they found both meditators and non-meditators were receiving pain signals, but meditators weren't translating them to actual feelings of pain. "We think that they feel the sensations, but cut the process short, refraining from interpreting or labeling the stimuli as painful," said Pierre Rainville, lead author of the study.[191]

Mindfulness meditation has also been shown to increase healing and boost the immune system.

- Kabat-Zinn taught mindfulness to a group of patients with psoriasis. Meditators' skin cleared up at a rate four times that of the non-meditators.[192]

- Kabat-Zinn with Richard Davidson administered flu shots to a group of newly trained meditators and non-meditators and then measured the anti-body levels. The meditators had more antibodies in their blood.[193]

- Another study reported, "women who meditate and use guided imagery have higher levels of immune cells known to combat tumors in the breast."[194]

- And Davison and Goleman report, "mindfulness training—even as short as three days—produces a short-term decrease in pro-inflammatory cytokines, the molecules responsible for inflammation. And the more you practice, the lower the level becomes of these pro-inflammatory cytokines."[195]

- Davidson and Goleman also report from their extensive review that, "a day long retreat by seasoned meditators benefited their immune response at the genetic level—a finding that startled the medical establishment."[196]

Meditation may even help get rid of pesky belly fat. Scientists at the University of California, San Francisco found a direct inverse relationship between meditation and the levels of the stress hormone cortisol.

So how do lower levels of cortisol target belly fat?

The answer lies in our evolutionary history. Our ancestors experienced extreme hardship when they faced famine and danger from predators. To compensate, humans evolved a stress-induced reaction that centrally stored fat in our stomachs and sides to survive starvation and stockpile energy. This deep-rooted process remains, leading us to eat and store fat when we are stressed. Cortisol is the hormone driving this response. So lower cortisol means less propensity to store fat.[197]

The *Journal of Nutrition Education & Behavior* offers another weapon for the "battle of the bulge." Mindfulness training helps people eat more slowly, consuming up to three hundred fewer calories in a day.[198]

In short, the health benefits of meditation have become widely accepted. And we now understand underlying mechanisms driving these benefits.

In 2013, researchers in Wisconsin, Spain, and France showed meditators change expression of genes. "To the best of our knowledge, this is the first paper that shows rapid alteration in gene expression within subjects associated with mindfulness meditation practice," stated Richard J. Davidson, William James Vilas Professor of Psychology and Psychiatry at the University of Wisconsin.[199] "Most interestingly, changes were observed in genes that are the targets of anti-inflammatory and analgesic drugs," said Perla Kaliman. She was first author of the journal article in *Psychoneuroendocrinology,* and a researcher at the Institute of Biomedical Research of Barcelona, Spain.[200] This helps explain mindfulness-based training benefits for inflammatory disorders.

We noted earlier Transcendental Meditation stimulates production of telomerase, an enzyme that helps rebuild protective caps allowing chromosomes to reproduce. So an increase in telomerase is naturally healthy and is felt to slow the aging process.[201]

Speaking of aging, our cerebral cortex shrinks with age. But here's the good news:

- A 2005 study showed people who meditated a mere forty minutes a day had thicker cortical walls than non-meditators.[202]

- Likewise, Sarah Lazar, PhD and assistant professor Harvard Medical School, in her Ted talk at Cambridge in 2011 demonstrated meditation's ability to make physical changes on our brain. Her studies showed a fifty-year-old who meditates has the same cortical mass as a twenty-five-year-old non-meditator.

- Another study done at UCLA found longtime meditators brains were "younger" by 7.5 years compared to the brains of non-meditators of the same age.[203]

For a summary on health benefits, the Mayo Clinic web page states it well: "Meditation can give you a sense of calm, peace and balance that benefits both your emotional well-being and your overall health. And these benefits don't end when your meditation session ends. Meditation can help carry you more calmly through your day and even improve certain medical conditions." The Mayo Clinic lists the following conditions that meditation could help: allergies, anxiety, asthma, binge eating, cancer, depression, fatigue, heart disease, high blood pressure, pain, sleep problems, and substance abuse.[204] More confirmation of "No. 1 Health Booster."

The Essence

Remember our reference to the Buddha and his "mind full of monkeys" analogy? That's the way the mind is. Its nature is to think, analyze, and compartmentalize.

When we are involved in activity or thought not requiring a mental effort, our brain's default mode is to hash over thoughts and feelings that focus on ourselves. When we meditate we *will have* these competing thoughts. But the goal, depending on the type of meditation, is to create more focus and develop mechanisms to internally acknowledge these thoughts and let them go. What we're doing is developing a "witness mind."[205]

The idea is to be aware of our thoughts and accept them, even though they are all over the place. But we also realize we can focus and choose. In the same way we do bicep curls to tone our arms, we exercise our brain to build focus or tone the muscle of the mind.[206] Meditation is, in fact, an active state of mind that generates brain waves associated with creativity and focus (depending on the type of meditation) and de-emphasizing those associated with other mental activity. We'll discuss further as we differentiate the types of meditation.

By comparing meditation to a physical workout we give the impression it can be a lot of work. Meditation does require effort, but not much. A study at Carnegie Mellon University found that brief mindfulness meditation, twenty-five minutes each day, alleviates psychological stress after just three consecutive days.[207]

Though types of meditation and methods for learning differ, benefits overlap. But scientists and doctors do recommend specific disciplines for certain issues, despite many commonalities. Yet few studies compare methods head to head.

So this ambiguity is a challenge as we search for the essence of a practice where methods are a lot alike, but they are different.

First, the old scientific myth that all meditation induces the same state of physiological rest, once called the "relaxation response," is not true.[208] Studies have debunked this theory.

However, all meditation paths have one thing in common: to notice when our mind has wandered and return to the chosen target, such as breathing, a mantra, or some other object of attention.[209]

Many of the contemplative paths also share the common goal of letting go of our thoughts, or diminishing the "stickiness" of our thoughts, a process called "dereification." According to Goleman and Davidson dereification provides a key insight: "thoughts, feelings, and impulses are passing, insubstantial mental events . . . we don't have to believe our thoughts; instead of following them down some track, we can let them go."[210]

Types of Meditation and Sources of Instruction

Though there are many types of meditation, most researchers agree on three major categories relating to instruction.

The first is **controlled focus meditation.** Subtypes within this category are Zen, Tibetan Buddhist, qigong, yogic and Vedantic. Attention is focused on an object of meditation such as one's breath, an image, or an emotion. This category is characterized by brainwaves typically in the gamma frequency associated with concentration or active cognitive processing. Research shows concentration on "loving-kindness and compassion" increases those feelings and produces synchronous gamma activity in the left prefrontal cortex, an indication of more powerful focus. [211]

The second major category is open monitoring, often called **"mindfulness,"** a practice common in **vipassana** as noted earlier. This practice involves actively paying attention or watching experiences or thoughts without judging, reacting or holding on.[212] Typical brainwaves are frontal theta, patterns seen during memory task or reflection on mental concepts. In addition, left frontal activity has been associated with positivity and happiness. Studies have proved mindfulness to be effective in pain management and reductions in negative ruminations. It's also been associated with stress reduction and attendant symptoms.[213]

The third major category is **automatic self-transcending.** The idea is to let the mind "spontaneously transcend the process of meditation itself."[214] A well-known example is **Transcendental Meditation.** In this approach no attempt is made to direct attention. Brainwaves associated with this category are frontal alpha coherence, characterized as a "distinct state of relaxed inner wakefulness."[215] This method is associated with relief from stress, lowering blood pressure, and alleviating chronic anxiety.

Think of mindfulness as surfing, and an awareness to move with the waves of your mind and maintaining that awareness. Transcendental Meditation is more like a submarine ride where you don't engage with the waves. You're striving for neither thought nor attention.[216] Whereas Transcendental Meditation and mindfulness are more associated with awareness, controlled focus is more deliberately concerned with concentration.

As we discuss methods for these types of meditation, you'll notice overlaps in technique, which indicate likely overlaps in function. In fact, some practitioners may well be going back and forth between meditation approaches. It's not a concern. Nevertheless, you may wish to learn the meditation most relevant to the result you are pursuing.

Cost may be a factor and we'll discuss in a moment.

Most practitioners say it's best to attend a class or get personal instruction. In fact, Transcendental Meditation is trademarked. To use the name and learn the method you must learn from a qualified teacher, with the price upwards of two thousand dollars.

To find an instructor go to TM.org and use the instructor locator. You'll also find much information and research about Transcendental Meditation. But there are practitioners who believe a version of mantra meditation is just as effective—for no cost. I cover a simple mantra meditation later in this chapter. On the other hand, many meditators swear taking the course is well worth the money. If you want the trademarked Transcendental Meditation, you must find an instructor and get out your pocketbook.

Mindfulness meditation classes are often taught in conjunction with larger hospitals. Just go to the web and search for MBSR courses in your area. For those who don't live near such facilities, the whole course is offered free at palousemindfulness.com/index.html.

"Mindfulness" and "mindfulness meditation" are complementary but can have slight variations in meaning. Mindfulness meditation involves sitting, focusing on your breath or other event and watching your thoughts with detachment. Mindfulness, on the other hand, has been adopted in psychology, therapy, and scientific research. Mindfulness meditation may be a part of mindfulness but mindfulness extends beyond the sit-down meditation to any daily activity.[217] You use the process to calm your mind in other activities by observing your own thoughts without judgment. Psychologists have made this practice the basis of mindfulness-based cognitive therapy, a method gaining rapid acceptance today.

A basic mindfulness meditation technique is provided below.

Controlled focus meditation can also be learned from an instructor—the most common being yoga. Yoga and qigong instructors are easily found on the web, or by asking around your community. You'll want to check references to make sure you are hiring a trustworthy instructor.

Another type of controlled focus meditation is compassion meditation, which is described in the following section.

Compassion Meditation

Below is a technique from Richard Davidson's highly recommended book *The Emotional Life of Your Brain*.

1. Start with visualizing a loved one at a time in their life when they were suffering.

2. With this image in mind next concentrate on a wish that the suffering end and silently repeating a phrase such as, "May you be free from suffering; may you experience joy and ease." Try to notice any slowing of heartbeat, stronger beating, or a warm sensation.

3. Then try to feel the compassion emotionally.

4. Next expand your "circle of compassion" in steps to yourself, then someone else you know, and on to someone you know of, but with whom you are not necessarily acquainted.

5. Finally go on to someone who may be a difficult person.[218]

Using this technique, Davidson found participants had decreased activation in the amygdala, the center of fear, and increased altruism or generosity when measured in lab experiments.

Mindfulness Meditation

Again, from Davidson, a simple mindfulness meditation is below, with elaboration from the Sam Harris web page on mindfulness meditation.[219] It all sounds so simple. And it is. But the process of witnessing your monkey brain at work will be a revelation!

1. Sit upright on a chair or the floor, keeping your spine straight in a relaxed but erect posture.

2. Take a few deep breaths. Focus on your breathing and the sensations triggered in your body. Notice how your abdomen moves in and out with each breath and the air flowing through your nostrils. There is no need to control your breath. Just let it come and go naturally.

3. Allow your attention to rest on the mere sensation of breathing. Find where you feel the breath most clearly, either at your nostrils or in the rising and falling of your abdomen.

4. When you notice you are distracted by an unrelated thought or feeling, acknowledge it (don't suppress) and then categorize it (such as a worry, plan, or miscellaneous thought) and then let it go. Then gently return your focus to your breathing.[220]

5. Continue as above until you can merely witness all objects of consciousness—sights, sounds, sensations, emotions, and even thoughts themselves—as they arise and pass through your consciousness and then away.

For added insight and elaboration, visit the following website: https//www.lionsroar.com/how-to-practice-Vepsian-meditation. Vipassana is considered the basis of mindfulness meditation. Or see Kabat-Zin's book, *Full Catastrophe Living,* as noted in the recommended reading section at the end of this appendix.

Mantra Meditation

Finally, a simple mantra meditation, sometimes considered similar to Transcendental Meditation:

1. On a chair or seated on the floor find your posture and center yourself and take several deep breaths.

2. Chant your mantra silently to yourself. Your mantra may be any word you wish or you can use the word *one* or the universal *OM*. Let your mantra find its own rhythm as you repeat it over and over.

3. The meditation is to be practiced with awareness. Try to stay aware of each repetition of the mantra.

4. When your thoughts stray, note that, then gently bring your attention back to your mantra.

After practicing any of these techniques for a while you will notice profound relaxation sensations. Recommendations vary about time for each session. A little is always better than none. Transcendental Meditation recommends twenty minutes twice a day. Mindfulness instructors say to start with five minutes and work up to forty minutes in a day. Remember, benefits accrue in as little as three days of practice, while two weeks can produce marked changes. Again, a course is recommended. It's always better to have personal feedback. If an in-person course is not possible, try the online courses, which provide significant detail.

A final word on comparison. Mindfulness meditation and mantra meditation (noted as a comparable to Transcendental Meditation) appear to be very similar. Though in one it's a matter of concentrating on the breath and the other a mantra, mindfulness instructors say you don't have to concentrate on your breath. It could be another bodily sensation or object. The difference comes down to handling the intrusive thoughts.

Mantra meditation has you simply returning to your mantra while mindfulness has you acknowledge and compartmentalize the thoughts before turning them loose, then returning to concentrating on your breath. The difference sounds menial. However, I can tell you from personal practice, the mindfulness method takes more effort. If more effort means better results and improved synapse building, that could be a reason to seek a good MBSR course or take a complete course online.

In summary, there are myriad reasons to meditate, and likely more we don't yet know. Sure, it will take twenty to forty minutes out of your day. But with the benefits, those twenty to forty minutes may be the most valuable of your waking hours

Recommended Reading on Meditation

1. *The Emotional Life of Your Brain* by Richard Davidson with Sharon Begley provides much more insight into various techniques and varying impact on the affective parts of your life. Happiness can be learned!

2. *Full Catastrophe Living* by Jon Kabat-Zinn is considered the handbook for MBSR courses and provides a full exploration of mindfulness.

3. *Altered Traits* by Daniel Goleman and Richard J. Davidson, published in 2018, features the two of the most widely known and respected scientists in the field. It applies rigorous scientific analysis to recent studies and explores meditation's ability to alter affective traits. Highly recommended.

APPENDIX II: RELIGION

"To them that ask, 'Where have you seen the gods, or how do you know for certain there are gods, that you are so devout in their worship?' I answer, 'Neither have I ever seen my own soul, and yet I respect and honor it.'"

–Marcus Aurelius

Wouldn't it be great if religion told us everything we need to know? Wouldn't it make life's decisions easier?

We do have religions making such claims. In the U.S. the extreme right evangelical Christians advance a political agenda of intolerance toward gays, immigrants, and, at times, Muslims. Likewise, Muslim extremist terrorists use horrible violence to inflict their religious beliefs on others. Unfortunately, this is not new in history. Consider the Crusades. We have reasons to believe that organized religions don't "get it right."

Most religions are exclusive, claiming to be the only true religion. If you don't believe in their doctrine, no eternal life for you! This is like saying God is only in one room and not others.

Then which religion is right? Who's wrong? How can we tell? Can we seek truth in the ancient scriptures that are the source of many of today's religions?

Seeking truth amid the underlying motives of the church means acknowledging time lapses between writings and events and realizing the likelihood of inaccuracies. Yet this doesn't mean there is no God. It just means the human beings, relaying their thoughts and observations, gave it their best shot but were as human as any of us in their capacity for error. And, since we are discussing a topic that is, by definition, beyond comprehension, how can we expect religious leaders to absolutely "get it right?"

Yet their efforts are not without fruit. People gathered together as a church can draw from one another and do great things for humanity. Perhaps the wise soul needs to be alert for the false teachings of humans but still be ready to absorb the essence of spirituality and be open to new discoveries of science in making sense of spirituality.

Our own upbringing weighs heavily on our perspective. Personally, I was raised Christian and try to follow the essence of Christ's teachings. Yet, I am wary of misinterpretations and, like Thomas Jefferson, I believe parts of the Bible cannot be true. (See Jefferson discussion below). And I have a problem with Christianity's exclusivist claim of being the only true religion. As described above, that's like saying God is in one room and not the other. And I certainly have a problem with the intolerance of right-wing Christians.

But that doesn't mean that the religion itself doesn't have a vital offering, if taken by the essence. I think of Christianity as being just one facet and one glimpse of a beautiful, multifaceted diamond. Other religions may provide another facet, again, taken by the essence and not necessarily by the doctrine of their leaders. If we could see through all facets, perhaps we could see the real beauty of the diamond.

But to review all religions is way beyond this exploration. However, we can explore the essence of one. By essence, I mean a truth contributing to our understanding of our condition as humanity, like the moral of the story.

For me, the most appropriate path is to use Christianity, the religion I was taught from childhood. But I am confident these principles apply to other religions.

Jesus Christ is one of the most famous, impactful persons to live on this planet. The Christian religion is the most popular on the planet with over two billion followers. Islam is second with 1.6 billion. (Muslims also acknowledge Christ and his teachings but relegate him to a prophet status.) So Christianity has, indeed, affected many lives. It is a message is of love, forgiveness, and salvation of our souls because of Christ's sacrifice of himself on the cross.

Most Christians believe Christ was the son of God and, therefore, our link to God. However, disagreement about interpretations of the Bible have spawned many Christian denominations and churches through the ages. Though Jesus walked the earth until about 30 AD, the earliest recountings of his teachings, or the gospels of the Bible, were not likely written until about 70 AD, soon enough for eyewitness recountings, but a long time for accurate memory. Biblical scholars have plenty to debate and research, but they universally agree that Christ did live and had a powerful impact on his followers.

One of the most famous forefathers of the U.S., Thomas Jefferson, had intense interest in the Bible. He believed Christ's teachings to be, "the most sublime and benevolent code of morals which has ever been offered to man." But he also studied it so carefully that he came to believe Christ's followers, who we assume wrote the gospels of the bible, combined Christ's gems of wisdom with their own political agendas. He didn't feel it was difficult to tell the difference. He took a razor blade and cut out parts he felt to be true and reassembled a slimmer, purer recounting of Christ's teachings. The old Bible with razor blade cuts has been on display at the National Museum of American History in Washington, D.C.

So how do we make sense of all this second-guessing? Who's right? Which interpretation is right? What is the truth?

When we ask such questions, we are implicitly asking for the most reliable guidance from the past or the empiricism of science. Though science is discovering the beauty of the universe, it is questionable that science can resolve issues of divinity that, by definition, are beyond our comprehension. Likewise, though science is assisting us in reconstructing history, it is doubtful that we'll ever be able to reconstruct exactly what happened two thousand years ago. And we have already seen how reliance on the past can keep us in a "world is flat" condition. Maybe it's more important to look within ourselves and our actions and results.

Christianity has been the basis for many alcoholics' recovery and has provided a source of great personal strength to many. We've all known people who have experienced healing or almost mystical experiences. Are these and many others truly the result of divine intervention or a benefit of the mind's orientation or religious training? Such thoughts will be eternally subject to question. But the benefit was there.

Christianity (as well as other religions) has also united people to accomplish great things. Check out the You Tube video "One Dallas 2016" or the movie *Woodlawn* for real-life examples of recent events.

Many people have found unification, peace, direction, and joy from Christ's teachings. Church missions have provided much aid to people in need. Many acts of kindness and love have been created. Human beings have the capacity to draw together for such acts of love.

As Jesus said, "God is Love." So people drawing together and creating acts of love are creating acts of divinity.

Jesus also said, "The Kingdom of God is within us." Perhaps that is literally true. Could not a detailed factual historical basis be *irrelevant* if the Kingdom of God is truly within us and followers can draw from each other to create acts of love? Perhaps our minds contain so much more capacity than we think.

Regarding the truth, perhaps one of the greatest essays is the editorial written by Francis Pharcellus Church in the September 21, 1897 edition of the New York *Sun*. It is history's most reprinted newspaper editorial. Church writes a reply to a little girl who asks if there is a Santa Claus. Here is the editorial:

DEAR EDITOR: I am 8 years old.
Some of my little friends say there is no Santa Claus.
Papa says, 'If you see it in THE SUN it's so.'
Please tell me the truth; is there a Santa Claus?

VIRGINIA O'HANLON.
115 WEST NINETY-FIFTH STREET

VIRGINIA, your little friends are wrong. They have been affected by the skepticism of a skeptical age. They do not believe except what they see. They think that nothing can be which is not comprehensible by their little minds. All minds, Virginia, whether they be men's or children's, are little. In this great universe of ours man is a mere insect, an ant, in his intellect, as compared with the boundless world about him, as measured by the intelligence capable of grasping the whole of truth and knowledge.

Yes, VIRGINIA, there is a Santa Claus. He exists as certainly as love and generosity and devotion exist, and you know that they abound and give to your life its highest beauty and joy. Alas! how dreary would be the world if there were no Santa Claus. It would be as dreary as if there were no VIRGINIAS. There would be no childlike faith then, no poetry, no romance to make tolerable this existence. We should have no enjoyment, except in sense and sight. The eternal light with which childhood fills the world would be extinguished.

Not believe in Santa Claus! You might as well not believe in fairies! You might get your papa to hire men to watch in all the chimneys on Christmas Eve to catch Santa Claus, but even if they did not see Santa Claus coming down, what would that prove? Nobody sees Santa Claus, but that is no sign that there is no Santa Claus. The most real things in the world are those that neither children nor men can see. Did you ever see fairies dancing on the lawn? Of course not, but that's no proof that they are not there. Nobody can conceive or imagine all the wonders there are unseen and unseeable in the world.

You may tear apart the baby's rattle and see what makes the noise inside, but there is a veil covering the unseen world which not the strongest man, nor even the united strength of all the strongest men that ever lived, could tear apart. Only faith, fancy, poetry, love, romance, can push aside that curtain and view and picture the supernal beauty and glory beyond. Is it all real? Ah, VIRGINIA, in all this world there is nothing else real and abiding.

No Santa Claus! Thank God! He lives, and he lives forever. A thousand years from now, Virginia, nay, ten times ten thousand years from now, he will continue to make glad the heart of childhood.

Hmmm. "Nobody can conceive or imagine all the wonders . . ." and ". . . there is a veil covering the unseen world . . . only faith, fancy, poetry, love, romance, can push aside that curtain and view and picture the supernatural beauty and glory beyond."

Maybe it's not what really happened two thousand plus years ago, but what does happen in lives of people who believe that stories such as those in the Bible can carry a greater truth and lead us to discovering higher truths within ourselves. And, perhaps this is the essence of Christianity and other religions as well.

NOTES

(Endnotes)

1   David Brooks, *The Social Animal: The Hidden Source of Love Character, and Achievement* (New York: Random House Trade Publications, 2011, 2012), 47.

2   Jason Zweig, *Your Money and Your Brain* (New York: Simon & Schuster Paperbacks, 2007), 60.

3   Jason Zweig, *Your Money and Your Brain*, 59.

4   Thomas Kida, *Don't Believe Everything You Think: The 6 Basic Mistakes We Make in Thinking* (Amherst, New York: Prometheus Books, 2006), 92.

5   Jason Zweig, *Your Money and Your Brain*, 61.

6   Ibid.

7   Sharon Begley, "Wanted BS Detectors, What Science Should Really Teach," *Newsweek*, November 6, 2010, 26.

8   Jason Zweig, *Your Money and Your Brain*, 61.

9   Ibid., 70.

10 Ibid., 80.

11 Ibid., 82.

12 Ibid., 82.

13 Amy Cater, "What's Missing in This Painting," *BottomLine Personal*, October1, 2016, 6

14 David Eagleman, "Secret Life of the Mind," *Discover*, September, 2011, 50.

15 Ibid., 94.

16 Jason Zweig, *Your Money and Your Brain*, 73.

17 Ibid., 73.

18 Ibid., 156.

19 Jason Zweig, *Your Money and Your Brain*, 111.

20 Gary Cokins, "Why Do Large, Once-Successful Companies Fail?" *Analytics Magazine*, June 20, 2012, accessed May 22, 2017, http;//www.analytics-magazine.org/corporate-decision-making-why-large-successfaul-companies-fail

21 Thomas Kida, *Don't Believe Everything You Think*, 104.

22 Darren Bridger, *Decoding the Irrational Consumer* (Philadelphia: Kogan Page Limited, 2015), 32.

23 Dan Ariely, *Predictably Irrational, Revised and Expanded Edition: The Hidden Forces That Shape Our Decisions*. (New York: Harper, 2008).

24 Ori Brafman and Rom Brafman, *Sway: The Irresistable Pull of Irrational Behavior* (New York: Broadway Books, 2008), 49.

25 Dan Ariely, "Societe Generale – behavior economics at work," February 1, 2008, accessed August 15, 2020, https://danariely.com/2008/02/01/societe-generale-behavior-economics-at-work/acc

26 Kathleen McGowan, "How Much of Your Memory Is True?" *Discover Magazine,* August 3, 2009, accessed May 17, 2017, http://discovermagazine.com/2009/jul-aug/03-how-much-of-your-memory-is-true

27 Ibid.

28 Ibid.

29 Ibid.

30 Gord Hotchkiss, "Pros And Cons Of A Fuel-Efficient Brain", June 19, 2014, accessed September 18, 2020, https:www.mediapost.com/publications/article/228388/pros_and_cons_of_a_fuel_efficient_brain.html?edition=73869

31 Ibid.

32 J. Keith Murnigham, "A Very Extreme Case of The Dollar Auction," *Journal of Management Education,* February 1, 2002, 56–69.

33 Ibid.

34 Sharon Begley, "I Can't Think," *Newsweek,* March 7, 2011, 28–33.

35 Ibid.

36 Ibid.

37 Jason Zweig, *Your Money and Your Brain,* 130.

38 Ibid., 131.

39 Ibid., 157.

40 Ibid., 163.

41 Ibid.

42 Thomas Kida, *Don't Believe Everything You Think,* 17.

43 John Gramlich, "5 Facts about Crime in the U.S.," Pew Research Center, October 17, 2019, accessed August 21, 2020, https:www.pewresearch.org/fact-tank/2019/10/17/5-facts-about-crime-in-the-u-s/

44 Zaid Jilani, "School Shootings Have Declined Dramatically Since the 1990's. Does It Really Make Sense to Militarize Schools?" *The Intercept,* March 1, 2018, accessed May 29, 2018. https://theintercept.com/2018/03/01/school-shooting-statistics-parkland-florida/

45 Nigel Barber, "Is the Modern World More Violent?" *The Human Beast,* June 30, 2015, accessed June 2, 2017, psychologytoday.com/blog/the-human-beast/201506/is-the-world-more-violent

46 Ibid.

47 Christopher Woolf, "The world is actually becoming more peaceful—believe it or not," PRI, September 29, 2014, accessed June 6, 2017, pri.org/2014-09-29/world-actually-becoming-more-peaceful-believe-it-or-not

48 Seth Borenstein, "In a Peaceful Place," *Rockford Register Star,* October 23, 2011, 3A.

49 Sharon Begley, "How the Brain Rewires Itself," *Time Magazine,* January 29, 2007, 73.

50 Sharon Begley, *Train Your Mind and Change Your Brain*, (New York: Balantine Books, 2008), 33.

51 Richard Davidson with Sharon Begley, *The Emotional Life of Your Brain* (New York: PLUME, 2013), 169.

52 Ibid., 169.

53 Begley, *Train Your Mind Change Your Brain*, 122.

54 Ibid., 54.

55 Ibid., 58.

56 Ibid., 63.

57 Ibid., 56.

58 Ibid., 66.

59 Ibid., 66–67.

60 Ibid., 69.

61 Begley, *Train Your Mind Change Your Brain*, 24.

62 Begley, "How the Brain Rewires Itself," 79.

63 Ibid.

64 Ibid., 79.

65 Richard E. Nesbitt, "Education Is All in Your Mind," *New York Times,* February 7, 2009, accessed November 26, 2018, https://www.nytimes.com/2009/02/08/opinion.08misbett.html

66 Donna Wilson, "Engaging Brains: How to Enhance Learning by Teaching Kids About Neuroplasticity," Edutopia, February 11, 2014, Accessed December 11, 2017, https://Edutopia.org/blog/neuroplasticity-engage-brains-enhance-learning-donna-wilson.

67 Peter Barnes, "What Is Neuroplasticity & How Does It Impact Education." The Learning Success Blog, September 5, 2016, accessed December 11, 2017, blog.learnfasthq.com/what-is-neuroplasticity-&-how-does-it-impact-education-infographic.

68 Lisa Flook and Laura Pinger, "Lessons from Creating a Kindness Curriculum," Center for Healthy Minds,Undated, accessed September 19,2020, https://centerhelathyminds.org/join-the-movement/lessons-from-creating-a-kindness-curriculum

69 Virginia Hughes, "Mice Inherit Specific Memories, Because Epigenetics?" December 1, 2013, *National Geographic, Only Human Blog*, accessed July 25, 2017, phenomena.nationalgeographic.com/2013/12/01/mice-inherit-specific-memories-because-epigenetics

70 Helmholtz Zentrum Muenchen – German Center for Environmental Health, "Lifestyle Influences Metabolism via DNA Methylation," *Science Daily*, September 20, 2013, Accessed August 14, 2017, sciencedaily.com/release/2013/09/130920094409.htm

71 Bruce H. Lipton, *The Biology of Belief, Unleashing the Power of Consciousness, Matter & Miracles* (Carsbad, California: Hay House, Inc, 2015).

72 University of Wisconsin-Madison, *Science Daily*, "Study Reveals gene expression changes with meditation," accessed January 2, 2017, sciencedaily.com/releases/2013/12/131208090343.htm

73 Frank Burns, "Brain Storm," *Madison Magazine*, November, 2007, accessed November 11, 2007, http://www.madisonmagazine.com/article.php?section_id=918&xstate=view_story&story

74 Ibid.

75 Sharon Begley, "Can You Build a Better Brain?" *Newsweek*, January 10 & 17, 2011, 45.

76 Danielle Braff, "7 Ways to Protect Your Memory," *Health Magazine*, September 19, 2012, accessed August 15, 2017, www.health.com/health/gallery/0,,20479128,00.html

77 Mandy Oaklander, "The New Science of Exercise," *TIME Health*, September12, 2016, accessed October 7, 2017, www.Time.com/4475628/the-new-science-of-exercise

78 Erin Brodwin, "There's even more evidence that one type of exercise is the closest thing to a miracle drug that we have," *Business Insider*, accessed December12, 2017, http://a.msn.com/05/en-us/BBGvcCX?ocid=se

79 Ibid.

80 Sharon Begley, "Can You Build a Better Brain?" *Newsweek*, January 10 & 17, 2011, 45.

81 Alex Hutchinson, "How Trees Calm Us Down," *The New Yorker*, July 23, 2015, accessed October 9, 2017, www.newyorker.com/tech/elements/what-is-a-tree-worth

82 Florence Williams, "This Is Your Brain on Nature," January, 2016, accessed 10-9-2017, Nationalgeographic.com/magazine/2016/01/call-to-wild

83 Dana Yates, "For Kids with ADHD, regular 'green time' is linked to milder symtoms," *Illinois News Bureau* blog, September 15, 2011, accessed October 16, 2017, news.illinois.edu/blog/view/6367/205232

84 Ephrat Livni, "The Japanese practice of 'forest bathing' is scientifically proven to improve your health," *Quartz*, October 12, 2016, accessed October 9, 2017, qz.com/804022/health-benefits-bathing

85 Rebecca Clay, "Green is good for you," April, 2001, accessed October 8, 2017, apa.org/monitor/apr01/greengood.aspx

86 Ibid.

87 Ibid.

88 MIkeala Conley, "Talking To Yourself May Help Your Brain," via ABC News – Good Morning America, April 24, 2012, accessed November 10, 2017, abcnews.go.com/Health/talking-to-yourself-may-help-your-brain/blogEnrty?id=16203493

89 Ibid., 158–159.

90 Joel Stein, "Just Say Ohm," 54.

91 "Research Summary: ADHD Meditation," ABC7 KGO-TV/DT, San Francisco, Oakland, San Jose, accessed June 18, 2006, http://abclocal. go.com/kgo/story?section=edell&id=4198564

92 Ibid.

93 Ibid.

94 "Eastern Philosophy Gains Acceptance In Bay State," The Boston Channel.com, accessed June 18, 2006, http://www.thebostonchannel.com/ print/9322474/detail.html

95 Ibid.

96 Liz Neporent, "Meditation Helps Kids Chill Out, Reduce Impulsivity," May 21, 2013, accessed February 6, 2017, gma.yahoo.com/meditation-helos-kids-chill-reduce-impulsiveness-021108463-abc-news-topstories.html

97 John Cloud, "Losing Focus? Studies Say Meditation May Help," Time. com, August 6, 2010, accessed February 6, 2017, http://www.sott.net/ article/213363-Losing-Focus-Studies-Say-Meditation-May-Help

98 Daniel Goleman & Richard Davidson, *Altered Traits,* 2017, Avery: New York, 251.

99 John Cloud, "Losing Focus? Studies Say Meditation May Help," Time. com, August 6, 2010, accessed February 6, 2017, http://www.sott.net/ article/213363-Losing-Focus-Studies-Say-Meditation-May-Help

100 Sandra Blakeslee, "Study Suggests Meditation Can Help Train Attention," *New York Times,* May 8, 2007, accessed 10-17-2017, http://psyphz.psych.wisc. edu/web/News/NYT_Med_0507.html

101 Daniel Goleman & Richard Davidson, *Altered Traits,* 2017, 282.

102 Ibid.

103 Welcome Trust, "Brain scans support findings that IQ can rise or fall significantly during adolescence," *Science Daily*, October 22, 2011, accessed July 8, 2019, https://www.sciencedaily.com/releases/2011/10/111020024329.htm

104 Daniel Goleman & Richard Davidson, *Altered Traits,* 2017, 282.

105 Editors, "Neuroplasticity: An extraordinary Discovery of the Twentieth Century," *A to Z of Brain, Mind, and Learning,* accessed 10-29-2017, www. learninginfo.org/neuroplasticity.htm

106 Sharon Begley, "Buff Your Brain," *Newsweek,* January 9 & 16, 2012, 35.

107 Tracy Shores, in "Speaking of Psychology: Keeping Your Brain Fit, Episode 28," interview by Audrey Hamilton, American Psychological Association, accessed December 26, 2017, www.apa.org/research/action/speaking-of-psychology/brain-fits.aspx

108 SharpBrains, "Build Your Cognitive Reserve: An Interview with Dr. Yaakov Stern," July 23, 2007, accessed October 18, 2017, sharpbrains.com/ blog/2007/07/23/build-your-cognitive-reserve-yaakov-stern

109 Ibid.

110 Chris Corrigall, "How Socializing Helps the Brain Function Better," February 20, 2015, accessed October 28, 2017, aegisliving.com/resource-center/how-socializing-helps-the-brain-function-better

111 Ibid.

112 Alvaro Frenandez and Dr. Elkhonon Goldberg, *The SharpBrains Guide to Brain Fitness*, SharpBrains, Inc., 2009, 145

113 Mark Prigg, "Laughing puts the brain into a 'true meditative state' AND can improve your memory, researchers claim," April 28, 2014, DailyMail.com, accessed October 28, 2017, dailymail.co.uk/sciencetech/article-2615351/Laughter-really-best-medicine-improve-memory-relaxing-meditating.html

114 Annie Drinkard, "Health Influenced by Social Relationsips at Work," October 3, 2016, SPSP, accessed November 6, 2017, spsp.org/news-center/press-release/health-social-relationships

115 Ibid.

116 Ibid.

117 Ibid.

118 "New Research: Meditation Changes Brain Physical Structure and Enhances Memory," PureInsight.org, accessed November 9, 2009, http://pureinsight.org/node/4737

119 "Meditation and success: Studies prove meditating leads to higher work efficiency," December 11,2015, accessed February 8, 2017, http://www.tmhome.com/benefits/meditation-work -performance-business-success.

120 Linda Wasmer Andrews, "6 Other Reasons to Meditate," *Psychology Today*, July 8, 2010, accessed February 1, 2017, http:www.psychologytoday.com/node/45123

121 Greater Good, "What is Mindfulness?," accessed September 29, 2016, www.greatergood.berkely.edu/topic/mindfulness/definition

122 Barbara Fredrickson, *Positivity*, (New York: Crown Publishing Group, 2009) 37.

123 Richard Davidson with Sharon Begley, *The Emotional Life of Your Brain*, (New York: Plume, 2012), 89.

124 Barbara Fredrickson, *Positivity*, 58.

125 Barbara Fredrickson, *Positivity*, 21.

126 Barbara Fredrickson, *Positivity*, 23.

127 Ibid., 27.

128 Ibid., 68.

129 Tom Rath and Donald O. Clifton, "The Power of Praise and Recognition," *Business Journal*, July 8, 2004, accessed April 4, 2018, news.gallop.com/businessjournal/12157/power-praise-recognition.aspx

130 Barbara Frerickson, *Positivity*, 27.

131 Ibid., 66, 92.

132 Ibid., 103.

133 Ibid., 108.

134 Richard Davidson with Sharon Begley, *The Emotional Life of Your Brain,* 127.

135 Susan Scutti, "Change Your Posture To Improve Your Mood, Memory, And 5 Other Aspects Of Your Life," *Healthy Living,* June 24, 2014, accessed September 23, 2018 https://www.medicaldaily.com/change-your-posture-improve-your-mood-memory-and-5-other-aspects-your-life-289724

136 Dave Munger blog, December 6, 2006, accessed December 7, 2007, www.scienceblogs.com/cognitivedaily/2006/12/06/depressed-think-faster-thought.

137 Ibid.

138 Maria Cheng, "Good Cheer May Spread Itself, a study suggests, Yahoo News, December 5, 2008, accessed December 6, 2008, http://news.yahoo.com/s/ap/20081205/ap_on_me/eu_med_contagious_happiness/print

139 Barbara Fredrickson, *Positivity,* 51.

140 Ibid., 161.

141 Gina Florio, "Science says this one habit can make you instantly happier today," accessed May 11, 2017, msn.com/en-us/healthtrending/science-says-this-one-habit-can-make-you-instatnly-happier-today/ar-BBAWTxo?li=BBmkt5R&ocid=spartandhp

142 Ibid.

143 Ibid.

144 Ryan J. Foley, "Scientist Inspired by Dalai Lama Studies Happiness," *The Oklahoman,* May 14, 2010, accessed January 29, 2018, www.newsok/article/feed/158821

145 Claudia Wallace, "The New Science of Happiness," *Time,* January 9, 2005, accessed December 4, 2007, www.time.com/time/printout/0,8816,1015902,00.html

146 Michael D. Lemonick, "The Biology of Joy," *Time,* January 9, 2005, accessed September 20, 2020, http://content.time.com/time/magazine/article/0,9171,1015863,00.html

147 Ibid.

148 Ibid.

149 Ibid.

150 Ibid.

151 Ibid.

152 Richard Davidson, "Be Happy Like a Monk," Lecture at Overture Center for the Arts, Madison, WI, February 13, 2007

153 Martin Seligman, "the pursuit of happiness," accessed January 16, 2018, www.pursuit-of-happiness-/martin-seligman-psychology/

154 Claudia Wallace, "The New Science of Happiness," *Time,* January 9, 2005, accessed December 4, 2007, www.time.com/time/ printout/0,8816,1015902,00.html

155 John Sentovich, letter from Northern Illinois University Foundation Cornerstone. April 16, 2009.

156 Kristina Ponischil. "Change Your Brain by Transforming Your Mind," March 27, 2014, accessed July 24, 2017, depts.washington.edu/ccfwb/ content/change-your-brain-transforming-your-mind

157 Richard Schiffman, "Can Kindness Be Taught?" *The New York Times,* December 14, 2017, accessed January 9, 2018, https://nyti.ms/2ksr9fo

158 Richard Davidson, "Be Happy Like A Monk," lecture held at Overture Center For the Arts, February 13, 2007, Madison, Wisconsin.

159 David Futrelle, "Here's How Money Really Can Buy You Happiness," *Time,* August 7, 2017, accessed April 13, 2018, Time.com/4856954/can-money-buy-you-happiness/

160 Ibid.

161 Ibid.

162 Ibid.

163 Jeffrey Kluger, "The Biology of Belief," *Time,* February 12, 2009, accessed July 27, 2009, www.time.com/printout/0.8816,1879016,00.html

164 Alvaro Fernandez and Elkhonon Goldberg with Pascale Michelon, *The SharpBrains Guide to Brain Fitness,* 2013, SharpBrains, Inc., 151

165 Virginia Sole-Smith, "The #1 Health-Booster in 2015," *Parade,* January 11, 2015, 11.

166 "Mindfulness Based Stress Reduction in Mind Body Medicine," accessed December 30, 2016, https://www.eomega.org/workshops/ mindfulness-based-stress-reduction-in-mind-body-medicine-2#-block-views-teachers-block-1,.

167 R. Morrissey, *Chicago Sun Times,* November3, 2016, 5.

168 Carolyn Gregoire, "The Daily Habit of These Outrageously Successful People," The Huffington Post, July 5, 2013, accessed December 27, 2016, huffingtonpost.com/2013/07/05/business-meditation-executives-meditation_n_3528731.html.

169 Ibid.

170 Sole-Smith, The #1 Health-Booster in 2015," 11.

171 Ibid.

172 Ibid.

173 Ibid.

174 University of Massachusetts Medical School, "Mindfulness-Based Stress Reduction Research Summary," accessed January 29, 2017, https://www. palousemindfulness.com/docs/research-summary.pdf

175 Ibid.

176 Ibid.

177 Ibid.

178 Ibid.

179 Daniel Goleman & Richard Davidson, *Altered Traits,* 2017, Avery: New York, 195

180 "Mindfulness-Based Stress Reduction in Medicine", accessed October 9, 2008, http://www.mindfullivingprograms.com/relatedresearch.php

181 Daniel Goleman & Richard Davidson, *Altered Traits,* 2017, 207

182 Laura Blue, "Strongest Study Yet Shows Meditation Can Lower Risk of Heart Attack and Stroke," *Time,* November 14,2012, accessed February 1, 2017, http://healthland.time.com/2012/11/14/mind-over-matter-strongest-study-yet-shows-meditation-can-lower-risk-of-heart-attack-and-stroke/

183 "Meditation benefits patients with heart disease," accessed June 18, 2006, http://www.brudirect.com/DailyInfo/News/Archive/June06/190606/wn03. htm

184 "Meta-analysis: Effect of TM™ on blood pressure," March 26, 2015, accessed Feb 1, 2017, https://www.tmhome.com/benefits/study-meditation-blood-pressure

185 Beyond medications and diet: Alternative approaches to lowering blood pressure, accessed January 29, 2017, http://www.tmhome.com/benefits/report-tm-lowers-blood-pressure

186 Linda Wasner Andrews, "6 Other Reasons to Meditate", *Psychology Today,* July 8, 2010, accessed February 1, 2017, http:www.psychologytoday.com/node/45123

187 Brian Vaszily, "A 20 Minute Vacation: The Amazing Health Benefits of Meditation," *Ezine @rticles,* accessed January 29, 2017, http://ezinearticles.com/?A-20-Minute-Vacation:-The-Amazing-Health-Benefits-of-Meditation&ID=91179

188 "New study on teacher stress and burnout," July 5, 2014, accessed January 29, 2017, http://www.tmhome.com/benefits/study-on-teacher-stress-and-teacher-burnout

189 Linda Wasner Andrews, "6 Other Reasons to Meditate", *Psychology Today,* July 8, 2010, accessed February 1, 2017, http:www.psychologytoday.com/node/45123

190 Adam Cole, "Even Beginners Can Curb Pain With Meditation," *NPR News,* April 8, 2011, accessed April 16, 2011, http://m.npr.org/news/front/135146672?singlePage=true

191 Meredith Melnick, "Mind Over Matter: Can Zen Meditation Help You Forget About Pain," December 9,2010, accessed February 5, 2017, http://www.healthland.time.com/2010/12/09/mind-over-matter-can-zen-meditation-help-you-forget-about-pain

192 Joel Stein, "Just Say Ohm," *Time,* August 4, 2003, 55.

193 Ibid.

194 Ibid.

195 Daniel Goleman & Richard Davidson, *Altered Traits*, 2017, 189.

196 Ibid., 253.

197 The Alternative Daily, "Does Meditation Help Fight Belly Fat?", accessed February 5, 2017, www.thealternativedaily.com/does-meditation-help-fight-body-fat

198 Sole-Smith, "The Number 1 Health-Booster in 2015," 12.

199 University of Wisconsin-Madison, "Study reveals gene expression changes with meditation," *Science Daily*, December 8, 2013, accessed January 2, 2017, http://www.sciencedaily.com/releases/2013/12/121208090343.htm

200 Ibid.

201 "New study: Transcendental Meditation™and lifestyle modification increase telomerase," December 6, 2015, accessed January 2, 2017, http://www.tmhome.com/benefits/study-tm-increase-telomerase

202 "Seven Fascinating Facts About Mindfulness," accessed February 5, 2017, rcpaconference.org/wp-content/uploads/2016/09/W54-Sallavanti-7-Fascinating-Facts-About-Minfulness.pdf

203 Daniel Goleman & Richard Davidson, *Altered Traits,* 2017, Avery: New York, 180.

204 Mayo Clinic staff, "Stress Management: Meditation: A simple, fast way to reduce stress," accessed November 10, 2011, http://www.mayoclinic.com/health/meditation/HQ01070

205 Amy Capetta, "How to calm your brain and find peace during a busy day," *Today*, accessed March 16, 2017, http://www.today.com/health/meditation-relieve-stress-anxiety-depression-be-happy-2D80161989

206 Ibid.

207 Shilo Rea, "Press Release: Only 25 Minutes of Mindfulness Meditation Alleviates Stress, According to Carnegie Mellon Researchers," Carnegie Mellon University, July 2, 2014, accessed March 21, 2017, http://www.cmu.edu/news/stories/archives/2014/july/july2_mindfulnessmeditation.html

208 Jeanne Ball, "How Meditation Techniques Comare-Zen, Mindfulness,Transcendental Meditation™ and more," The Blog, Huffingtonpost.com, November 17, 2011, accessed November 7, 2016, http://www.huffingtonpost.com/how-meditation-techniques_b_735561.html

209 Daniel Goleman and Richard Davidson, *Altered Traits*, 2017, 152.

210 Ibid., 153.

211 Ibid.

212 Ibid.

213 Ibid.

214 Ibid.

215 Ibid.

216 The Diane Rehm Show, May 17, 2016, transcript accessed December 29, 2016, http://www.thedianerehmshow.org/shows/2016-05-17/mindfulness-and-transcendental-meditation-why-these-practices-are having-a-moment

217 Mathew Young, "What is the difference between mindfulness and meditation?", February 10, 2014, accessed November 7, 2016, http://www.melbournemeditationcentre.com.au/article/what-is-the-difference-between-mindfulness-and-meditation

218 Richard J. Davidson with Sharon Begley, *The Emotional Life of Your Brain,* January, 2013, Plume, London, 221.

219 Sam Harris, "How To Meditate," May 10, 2011, SamHarris.org, accessed January 11, 2018. https://www.samharris.org/blog/item/how-to-meditate

220 Ibid., 234.